COCINA HOLISTICA

Plant-Powered Recipes Inspired by Guatemalan Superfoods

COCINA HOLISTICA

Plant-Powered Recipes Inspired by Guatemalan Superfoods

KASSIA EMILY FIEDOR

VERIDITAS PUBLISHING

Copyright © 2019 by Kassia Emily Fiedor

All rights reserved. No part of this book may be reproduced or used in any manner without written permission of the copyright owner except for the use of quotations in a book review. For more information, write info@infusedholistickitchen.com.

Book design by Kassia Emily Fiedor
Cover design by Kassia Emily Fiedor & Alyssa Hyndman
Original Concept & Co-Production Lucia Barrios
Co-Production Kassia Emily Fiedor
Principle photography by Mono del Espacio
Map by Charlie Hyndman

Published by Veriditas Publishing
www.infusedholistickitchen.com
@infusedholistickitchen

ISBN 978-0-578-45029-2 (paperback)

First paperback edition March 2019

Dedicated to the spirit of Guatemala,
for welcoming me with an open & generous heart.

INTRODUCTION page 9

1 | BREAKFASTS page 13

2 | SOUPS page 29

3 | SALADS page 45

4 | MAINS page 59

5 | SNACKS page 91

6 | FERMENTS page 109

7 | DESSERTS page 133

8 | DRINKS page 155

FEATURED FARMS page 181
ACKNOWLEDGMENTS page 186
INDEX page 188
BIBLIOGRAPHY page 190

Introduction

I bet you're wondering - why a cookbook about Guatemala? Like everything in life, a string of synchronistic events lead me to that magical country, and the next thing I knew, I had a full-on life there. The moment I planted roots, they immediately flourished into 5 years of adventure, friendship, beauty, love, pain, forgiveness, challenge, and personal growth. I feel as though I lived a lifetime in those 5 years, blessed with a whirlwind of incredible experiences in a seemingly random place. Isn't this the key to life, to live with a heart open to all possibilities? I never imagined my path would lead me to Guatemala, but now I know I was exactly where I was meant to be. This cookbook is a snapshot of all the experiences that came together to define my life's purpose of working with food as medicine.

I've always had a passion for the natural world and having grown up in a remote area of San Diego, I was given the chance to explore that world deeply. As a child, I would ride my horse through the desert trails of white sage, buckwheat, manzanita, and oak trees. Often discovering metates ground into the huge granite boulders near my childhood home, I felt the Native American Kumeyaay ancestors close by and imagined them living among those beautiful hills. I couldn't help but wonder how they survived that dry climate - which plants did they use as medicine and food? Growing up close to the earth planted the seed for my reverence for nature, and gave me an insatiable curiosity about native plants used by our ancestors around the world.

What ultimately guided me onto the holistic path was a horrible battle with acne in my teens and early adulthood. I had somehow developed a very strong phobia of doctors, hospitals, and shots as a child and one particular interaction with a doctor left a profound imprint on me. At age 15 my acne was raging, and my parents took me to a dermatologist to get some help. With barely a glance at my face and no questions asked, the doctor was handing me a prescription for antibiotics, clearly ending the appointment. I still vividly remember feeling like just a number, not a human being. Weren't doctors supposed to make you feel cared for? How did she know this treatment was right for me? Wouldn't it make sense to get more information about my lifestyle, my diet, my stress, my activities, my skincare regimen? This is the moment I lost faith in western medicine as the answer to true health and started seeking a more holistic and empowered approach to wellness.

I started casually exploring the plants in my backyard, making medicinal teas and herbal masks to calm my skin. I didn't know what I was doing, and without the extensive interwebs we have now I relied on the few herb books I could find. After high school, I went to college for my bachelors in Psychology. It wasn't until years later, after traveling the world and living a life of freedom and adventure, that I finally dove deep into the plant path. I was a vegetarian all of my childhood and into my 20's, so I had been experimenting with vegetables and health trends - from raw food to juice fasting - for years. I was feeling a strong call to nutrition and herbs all of this time yet I didn't know how to pursue it. Although I was happy and carefree I felt lost in the world without direction. I finally realized the only choice I had was to follow that intuitive pull toward nutrition, food, and plants, which I came to understand was my divine purpose.

We are all born with our own seed of innate wisdom to activate our higher purpose - just as the acorn emerges into an oak. Studying Holistic Nutrition at Bauman College in Berkeley was my first conscious decision to align with this purpose, and from then on I was living in my flow. I learned to cook at Three Stone Hearth, a community supported kitchen focused on nutrient-dense, healing foods and a commitment to using only the highest vibration ingredients. Working at Three Stone helped me embody the meaning of holistic - that supporting our own health with high quality, organic, local food grown with love means also supporting the planet.

I started offering services as a private chef in San Francisco and my business took off. It was challenging for me yet felt so good to be doing what I loved - healing people through food! It was only natural for me to pursue medicinal herbs as the next step in my plant path. The California School of Herbal Studies in Northern California had an incredible experiential program and a flourishing garden to get to know all my new herb friends. It was during this program that my soul felt at home - and the universe confirmed this with an opportunity to co-own a beautiful herb shop in Marin County. I felt like the luckiest girl in the world. I got the chance to work alongside Cheryl Fromholzer, a very talented herbalist, and was blessed to learn from her every day while serving my community with herbal medicine!

I loved my herb shop so much but the Universe had other plans for me. My husband at the time worked for USAID and was assigned to work in Guatemala. One year after we moved there, he came out of the closet and we got divorced. My life turned upside down, to say the least, but I had already invested so much into my life in Guatemala, so I stayed. I was faced with the challenge of starting my own business in a foreign country, not yet fully confident speaking Spanish, all while grieving. The country and its people welcomed me with open arms and opportunities to thrive doing what I loved. This was my chance to gather all of my knowledge of food, herbs, and nutrition and put it into practice in a country that really needed it! I cooked for people who appreciated organic food prepared with love and gave healthy private cooking classes. I dove into the rich culture of Guatemala, investigated what wild herbs the Mayans used, and obsessively searched out farmers growing native foods using ancient and organic practices. It became my passion to incorporate indigenous ingredients into my healthy style of cooking, to make these ancestral foods exciting again in a country that glorifies imports from the US.

This cookbook is a love letter to Guatemala;

a thank you for healing my heart. She offers so much abundance yet many have forgotten their connection to the plants there that have the ability to nourish and heal. My goal is to revitalize that connection through inventive and modern recipes that celebrate these native ingredients. I invite Guatemalans to explore all the ancient superfoods growing in their country and to support the farmers and artisans cultivating a connection between food, nature, and health. I hope to inspire renewed respect for indigenous foods around the globe. No matter our lineage, these native plants have the capacity to connect us to each other and to our roots. The awareness of this connection is deeply rooted in the psyche of all ancient cultures, and once you embody this, you realize we are all one. Every time we put something into our bodies we have a choice - to choose between foods that will nourish us, give us energy, prevent disease, and support the environment or foods that will feed disease, promote inflammation, and harm the planet. My philosophy is simple - listen to your body, incorporate more whole foods into your diet, and make wellness a lifestyle. I hope this book leaves you with a glimpse of how food can truly be a source of healing for us & for Gaia.

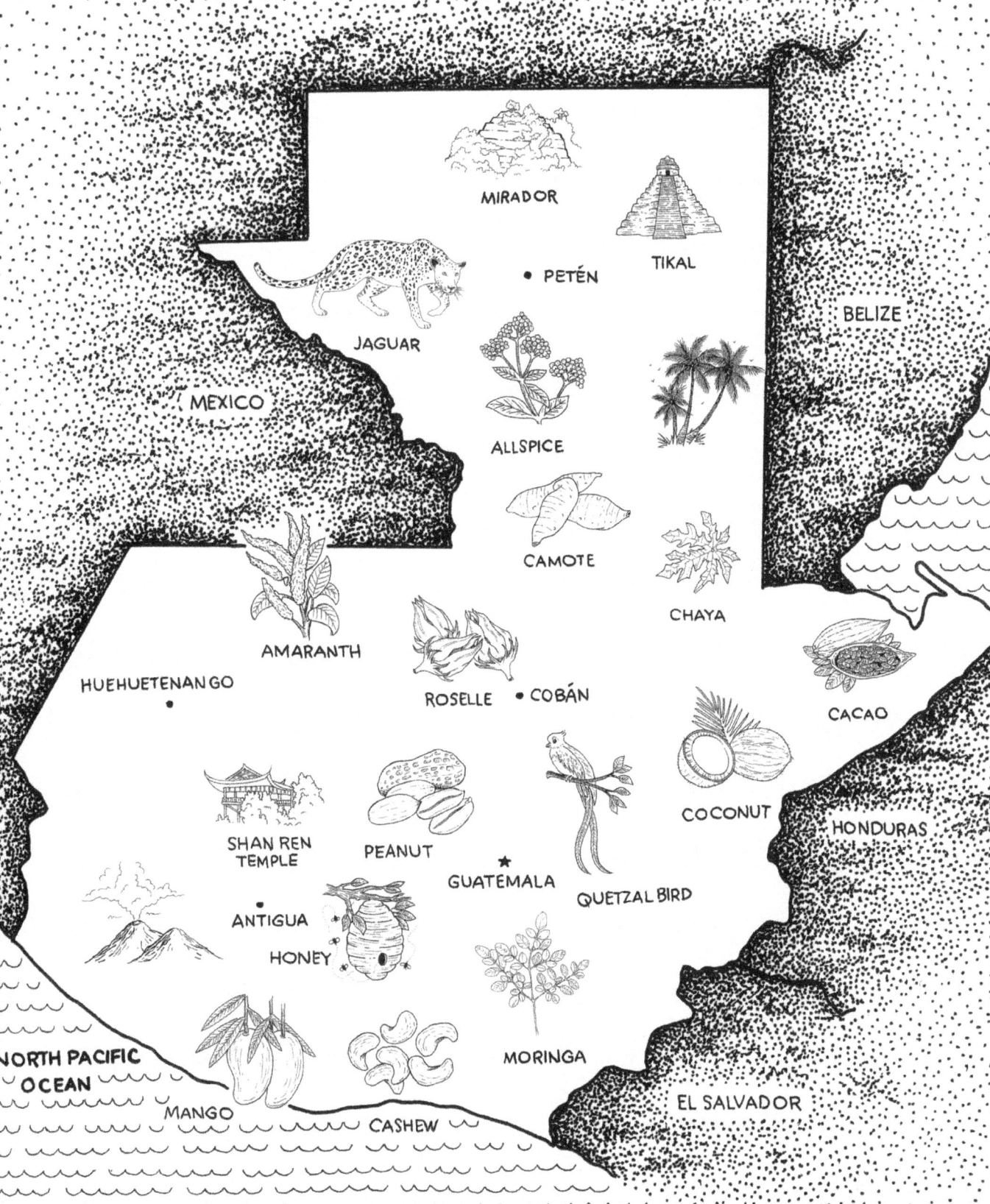

1

Breakfasts

Chipilín Shakshuka

Amaranth Pancakes with Cardamom Hibiscus Cream

Amaranth Camote Porridge

Pltaya Chia Pudding

Tamarillo Amaranth Crumble

Chipilín Shakshuka

Serves 4

I'm a gypsy – exotic lands intrigue me, and I'm blessed to have experienced many different cultures. Upon writing this book, I have yet to visit North Africa, where this trendy dish originates, so why not put my spin on it?

Traditional Shakshuka is eggs poached in tomatoes, peppers, and spices. The key to this dish is patience – cooking it "slow and low," allowing the onion to caramelize and the sweetness of the peppers and tomatoes to unfold. I use a generous amount of coconut oil, which is one of the world's healthiest fats – it boosts your metabolism and is a super fuel for your cells, supports brain and thyroid health, aids in digestion, and balances hormones. I like to use one bell pepper and one of its Guatemalan cousins, the "chile pimiento." I sneak greens into everything, so a touch of native chipilín leaf lends its delicate flavor plus vitamins A, C, calcium, and beta-carotene.

¼ cup coconut oil
1 large yellow onion, large dice
1 bell pepper (yellow, orange, or red), sliced into 1 inch strips
1 chile pimiento (or an extra bell pepper), sliced into 1 inch strips
6 ripe tomatoes, large dice
4 garlic cloves, finely chopped
1 teaspoon paprika, ground

2 tablespoons cumin, ground
1 teaspoon coriander, ground
pinch of chili cobanero (or cayenne)
salt to taste
1-2 cups water to thin
½ cup chipilín leaves, chopped
¼ cup parsley, chopped
4-6 eggs

- In a very large skillet, heat oil and add onions and 1 teaspoon salt. Sauté 20 minutes on low heat, stirring often.

- Add the peppers, tomatoes, garlic, and spices and simmer on low heat 30 minutes. Add water while simmering the veggies to create a pasta sauce consistency.

- When everything has cooked down, add chipilín and half the parsley, mix well.

- Make little gaps in the mixture, then break an egg into each gap. Cover and simmer on low for about 10 minutes, until eggs are set. Sprinkle with remaining parsley, and serve.

Serve this to guests for brunch and they will be impressed!

Amaranth Pancakes
with cardamom hibiscus cashew cream

Makes 8 small pancakes

Channel the strength of the Mayans by starting your day with these fluffy gluten-free pancakes! Amaranth has endured the threat of near extinction, and is now taking center stage as the "grain of the future." Actually a seed, this tiny superfood was so sacred to Mesoamerican ancestors for its nutrient density that it was used in religious ceremonies and even considered a deity in some areas. When colonizing Catholics caught wind of this, it was banned. In Guatemala, it resurfaced, but those cultivating it during the Civil War were oppressed and again it was nearly lost. I visited a group of indigenous Mayan widows who had lost their husbands in the war and are now successfully rebuilding (and nourishing) their villages by cultivating and selling their organic amaranth. This story imbues the humble amaranth seed with an essence of empowerment and transformation!

DRY INGREDIENTS

¼ cup amaranth flour

2 tablespoons + 1 teaspoon coconut flour (do not substitute)

1 teaspoon spices (cinnamon, cloves, ginger, and/or cardamom)

½ teaspoon baking powder

2 pinches of salt

WET INGREDIENTS

¼ cup coconut milk

3 eggs

1 tablespoon honey

1 teaspoon apple cider vinegar

CASHEW CREAM

½ cup dried hibiscus flowers (or powdered hibiscus)

½ cup boiling water

¼ cup raw cashews

1 drop orange essential oil (or zest of ½ orange)

juice of 1 orange

1 tablespoon maple syrup

¼ teaspoon cardamom

pinch of salt

Amaranth fields

Amaranth Pancakes cont....

- Steep hibiscus in boiling water for about 10 minutes. (if using powdered hibiscus, skip this step, and simply add everything to the blender).
- Meanwhile add cashews, orange zest and juice, maple syrup, cardamom, and salt to a high-speed blender.
- Strain the hibiscus infusion (liquid portion) into the blender, and blend until smooth. Adjust sweetness and flavors to your liking.
- In a medium bowl, combine all the dry ingredients. In a small bowl or cup, mix all the wet ingredients until the eggs are fully whisked. Add the egg mixture to the flour mixture, and stir well until you have an incorporated batter.
- Heat a medium size skillet or griddle to medium-low heat, and add in a tablespoon of butter or coconut oil.
- When the oil is hot, pour the batter onto the griddle, using about ¼ cup for each pancake. Cook until golden brown on both sides.
- Serve with hibiscus cashew cream and/or maple syrup.

Amaranth Camote Porridge

Serves 3

Often considered a grain, amaranth is in fact a seed that has fortunately experienced a rebirth in popularity lately. Nearly forgotten at one point in history, this nutrient powerhouse was very sacred to the ancient Mayans who used it not only as a staple in their diets, but also in religious ceremonies. This tiny seed packs a huge protein punch including high levels of antiviral lysine, and significantly more calcium than milk. Amaranth also contains high amounts of tocotrienols, counterparts of vitamin E rarely found in plants which have powerful neuroprotective, anti-tumor, antioxidant, and cholesterol lowering properties. This incredible ancient seed combined with coconut milk, the beloved Guatemalan camote sweet potato, and warming spices is the perfect breakfast for a chilly morning. I love to blend in maca for an extra energy boost and serve it topped with more coconut milk, orange zest, maple syrup, and toasted coconut.

½ cup whole grain amaranth
1 cup full fat coconut milk
½ cup water
¼ teaspoon salt
½ teaspoon grated ginger

¾ teaspoon ground cinnamon
pinch of ground allspice
1 teaspoon powdered maca
1 cup camote or sweet potato, chopped into ½ inch squares

- Drain and rinse amaranth.
- In a small pot, combine amaranth with coconut milk, water, salt, spices, and maca. Bring to a boil, cover, and simmer on low for 15 minutes.
- Stir in the camote, and simmer another 15 minutes. Add a bit more milk to thin the texture out if desired.
- Top with maple syrup, more coconut milk, orange zest, and toasted coconut.

Pitaya Chia Pudding

Serves 3

This breakfast favorite gets its vibrant color from pitaya, the exotic tropical fruit that grows on cactus. Also known as Dragon fruit, it is native to Central America, and contains a powerhouse of antioxidants, vitamin C & A, magnesium, and calcium. The double dose of omega-3's from the tiny black seeds of the pitaya plus the chia make this pudding heart healthy. I tend to like my chia pudding thinner than others, so if you prefer a thick consistency, add 1 more tablespoon of chia. Tip – chop and freeze your pitaya so you can enjoy this all year long!

1 cup macadamia milk (or your favorite non-dairy milk)
½ cup pitaya (about 1 pitaya fruit)
2 teaspoons lime juice
honey or agave to taste (about 1-2 tablespoons)

½ teaspoon shredded ginger
1 tablespoon shredded coconut
3 tablespoons chia seed

- Blend the milk, pitaya, lime, honey/agave, and ginger until you have a smooth consistency.
- In a Tupperware with a secure lid, pour in the mixture and add the chia seed and shredded coconut.
- Quickly cover with the lid, then shake until the chia and coconut are incorporated.
- Store in the fridge a few hours or overnight, until it thickens. Serve topped with your favorite nuts and superfoods.

Tamarillo Amaranth Crumble

Serves 6

Otherwise known as tree tomato or tamarillo, "tomate de arbol" is one of my favorite fruits in Guatemala. Native to Central and South America, they are mostly found in home gardens and backyards, and surprisingly they're grown commercially in New Zealand. They're in the Nightshade family, related to tomatoes and eggplants. High in vitamins A, C, E, and B6, as well as fiber, this fruit is tangy and sweet, making it perfect for a crumble. To easily peel off the bitter skin, score an X into the tip of each tomate de arbol with a knife. Simmer in hot water for 10 minutes, then peel. This would be a nice low-sugar dessert, breakfast, or snack. If you don't have access to tamarillos, substitute any sour fruit or even rhubarb.

CRUST

- 1 ½ cups rolled oats
- 1 cup pecans
- 3 tablespoons coconut oil
- 1 egg
- 3 tablespoons honey
- ¼ teaspoon salt

FILLING

- 10 tomates de arbol, peeled (≈ 6 cups)
- ½ cup dates, soaked in hot water 20 mins
- 1 tablespoon chia seeds
- pinch of salt

CRUMBLE

- 1 cup amaranth flour
- ½ cup oats
- 1/3 cup shredded coconut
- ¼ cup honey or maple syrup
- 1 teaspoon cinnamon
- 1 teaspoon cardamom
- 1 teaspoon dried ginger
- 4 tablespoons (half stick) butter, cold, and cut into small squares
- ¼ teaspoon salt

- Preheat oven to 350°F.
- In a food processor, blend oats and pecans until you have a rough flour. Add coconut oil, egg, honey, and salt. Pulse until you have the texture of dough.

Tomate de arbol, or tamarillo, is a sweet and tangy fruit native to Central and South America, and high in vitamins A, C, E, and B6.

Tamarillo Amaranth Crumble cont....

- Place the dough into a lightly greased 8"x8" brownie pan and press firmly. It helps to wet your hands so that the dough doesn't stick. Place in the oven for 20 minutes.

- To make the filling, place the tomates de arbol, dates, and salt in a blender and blend until smooth. Add the chia seeds at the last minute, and pulse quickly to combine.

- Remove the crust from the oven and spread all of the filling over it.

- In a medium bowl, mix the ingredients for the crumble, using your fingers to incorporate the butter.

- Sprinkle the crumble topping over the layer of filling.

- Place in the oven for 15 minutes, until slightly golden on top.

- Let cool completely before cutting into bars.

- Serve with coconut cream, vanilla ice cream, or coconut butter if desired.

- Store in the fridge for up to five days.

2

Soups

Creamy Tomato Basil Soup

Carrot Camote Ginger Soup

Ichintal Güicoyito Soup

Immunity Soup

Creamy Tomato Basil Soup

Serves 4

If you love tomato soup, this will become your new favorite. It's creamy, rich, and well-balanced. I roast the tomatoes not only to bring a rich depth of flavor to the soup, but also because lycopene, the anti-cancer antioxidant found in tomatoes, is better utilized by the body when it's cooked. Lycopene is a fat-soluble nutrient, so the healthy fats in the macadamias ensure its absorption and also lend a creamy texture. I love to use the local spicy Guatemalan basil "albahaca morada," but any basil will work!

4 tomatoes, roasted until black (or sub 1 14.5 oz can diced fire-roasted)
½ cup sundried tomatoes
½ cup macadamia nuts (or cashews)
¼ cup basil, packed
4 cups water

1 garlic clove
1 tablespoon lime juice
2 tablespoons olive oil
½ teaspoon black pepper
1 teaspoon sea salt

- Preheat the oven to 500° F (broil).
- Place the tomatoes in a Pyrex or small sheet pan and broil until blackened, rotating once.
- Meanwhile, add everything else to a high-speed blender.
- When the tomatoes are done, peel off the black skins, and place the tomatoes in the blender.
- Blend everything until creamy and smooth. Taste and adjust salt and lime.

Camote Carrot Ginger Soup

Serves 4

There are many carrot ginger soups out there, but this one stands out as a winner. I like to use camote – Guatemala's most iconic and adored vegetable. These sweet potatoes have been a staple of the Mesoamerican diet for thousands of years, and still can be found in nearly every Guatemalan kitchen and market today. They're a fabulous source of fiber, antioxidants, vitamins, and minerals, particularly beta-carotene and vitamin A. Camote are not as sweet as the sweet potato variety we find in the states, but either will work well in this soup. The variety of spices make this creamy, flavor-packed soup super versatile – serve it alongside any Thai, Mexican, or Indian main dish.

- 2 tablespoons coconut oil
- 1 large onion, chopped
- 2 garlic cloves, chopped
- 1 jalapeno, seeds removed, chopped
- 2 teaspoons thyme
- 2 inch piece of ginger, chopped
- 2 tablespoons cumin, ground
- 3 cups vegetable or chicken broth
- 1 can full-fat coconut milk
- 1 cup carrot, chopped in 1-inch cubes
- 1 cup camote, chopped in 1-inch cubes (or regular sweet potato)
- 1 tablespoon honey
- juice of 1 lemon
- 2 teaspoons sea salt
- chopped cilantro to serve
- toasted pumpkin seeds, to serve
- dollop of yogurt, crème fraische, or coconut milk to serve

- In a large stock pot, heat coconut oil on low heat, then add onions with 1 teaspoon salt. Allow to caramelize, about 20 minutes, stirring occasionally.
- Add garlic, jalapeno, thyme, ginger, and cumin, stir to combine. When spices become aromatic, add broth, coconut milk, carrot, and camote, bring to a boil.

- Reduce heat, and allow to cook, covered, until the carrot and camote are soft, about 20 minutes.
- Allow to cool a little, then add to a high-powered blender, along with the honey, lemon, and salt. Blend until very smooth. Taste, and adjust seasonings by adding more salt, lime, or cumin.
- Serve with chopped cilantro, yogurt or cream, and toasted pumpkin seeds.

Camote, Guatemala's sweet potato

Ichintal Güicoyito Soup

Serves 4

This green soup features three main ingredients that have deep ancestral roots in Guatemala - güicoyitos, ichintal, and macuy. Ichintal, the root of the chayote or güisquil plant, was a staple in Pre-Colonial diets and is said to control high blood pressure. Considered a delicacy, ichintal is incredibly rich and soft when cooked, resembling the texture of a potato and lends a nice creaminess to the soup. Native macuy leaves are rich in iron, protein, and phosphorus and contain anti-fungal compounds helpful for skin conditions. Güicoyitos are cute Mayan heirloom squash that look and taste like round zucchini. If you don't have access to these vegetables, substitute potatoes or cauliflower for ichintal, zucchini for güicoyitos, or spinach for macuy. Sip this soup and travel back in time to the ancient civilizations of Mesoamerica.

2 tablespoons coconut oil
1 onion, chopped
3 garlic cloves, chopped
2 celery stalks, chopped
2 cups güicoyitos, cubed
1 teaspoon ground cumin

1 cup ichintal, cubed
3 cups vegetable broth, chicken broth, or water
1 cup macuy, rough chopped
1 teaspoon sea salt
juice of ½ lemon

- In a large stock pot, heat the oil on low heat, then add the onion and celery and a teaspoon of salt. Allow the onions and celery to simmer, stirring occasionally. They should be simmering slowly, but not burning.

- Once they have started browning (this gives a lot of flavor), add the garlic, guicoyitos, and cumin, and stir about 2 minutes.

- Add the ichintal root and the broth or water. Bring to a boil, then lower the heat, and simmer uncovered about 15 minutes, until the veggies have softened.

- Turn off the heat, then add the macuy, allowing it to wilt a few minutes.

- Add everything plus the lemon juice to a high-speed blender, and blend until smooth. Adjust the flavors - add more salt, lemon juice, or cumin to your liking.

Macuy, sometimes referred to as quilete or hierba mora, is a nutritious weed found in most Guatemalan markets.

Immunity Soup

Serves 4

Sometimes even herbalists get sick! During those times, I try my darndest to remind myself that it's my body's way of resetting and that I'm blessed to have the knowledge and tools to get back on the healing path. One fall in Nashville, I got a respiratory infection that knocked me down for a few weeks. Being a Cali girl new to this southern climate, my immune system was vulnerable to changes of season and exposure to foreign pathogens, central heating systems, and unfamiliar pollen. None of my herbal medicines were working, and I was starting to lose hope. When I could muster the energy to cook, I made up a huge batch of this powerful soup, drawing inspiration from Traditional Chinese Medicine. The approach is to use warming spices and immune boosting foods to create internal heat, and sweat the infection out. After bundling up and sipping this soup, my body knew just what to do with the nourishment, and I was on the road to recovery in no time.

- 2 tablespoons coconut oil
- ½ cup shallots or red onion, chopped
- 1 teaspoon salt
- 2 teaspoons fresh turmeric, in slices, or 1 teaspoon powdered
- 4 garlic cloves, minced
- 1 quart chicken or veggie broth
- ½ cup coconut milk
- 3 bulbs fresh lemongrass, tough outer layers removed, minced
- 2 inch piece of ginger, in slices
- 2 green onion, sliced, green and white parts
- 3 cups of shiitake mushrooms, chopped into bite sizes
- handful chopped greens – spinach, collards, chard, kale, watercress
- 3 tablespoons white mellow miso
- 1 tablespoon lemon juice
- ¼ teaspoon black pepper

- In a large stock pot, heat coconut oil on medium-low heat, then add shallots and salt. Allow to caramelize a bit, about 15 minutes.

- Add turmeric and garlic, sauté a few minutes until fragrant.

Immunity Soup cont....

- Add broth, coconut milk, lemongrass, ginger, and half the green onions.
- Bring to a boil, then reduce heat and cover, simmering for 15 minutes.
- Add the mushrooms, and simmer another 5 minutes.
- Remove from heat, and add greens, miso, lemon juice, and black pepper.
- Adjust flavors, adding more salt, miso, or lemon to taste. Leave the large slices of ginger & turmeric to infuse as you eat the soup over the next few days, or remove if desired.
- Serve hot, breathing in the healing steam.

In some Native languages the term for plants translates to "those who take care of us."

— **Robin Wall Kimmerer**, *Braiding Sweetgrass*

3

Salads

Green Mango Coconut Salad

Watercress Mandarin Salad with Turmeric Vinaigrette

Arugula Camote Salad with Loroco Ranch

When we have life giving positive thoughts about nourishing ourselves we are more deeply nourished & fed by our food.

- Brittany Wood

Green Mango Coco Salad

Serves 4-5

This salad is so refreshing and cooling! Inspired by the Thai Papaya Salad, I gave it my healthy twist by balancing flavor and nutrition. Green (unripe) mangos are a low glycemic fruit high in vitamins C, A, and B6. The fiber and enzymes are great for digestion. The herbs in this salad add a boost of antioxidant power, while the coconut provides healthy fats that are burned quickly for energy. This dressing is a perfectly balanced creamy blend of spicy and sweet - if you don't like spicy, simply omit the chile.

SALAD

- 1 green mango, julienned (or shredded)
- ½ red onion, sliced thin
- ½ young coconut, sliced into thin strips
- 1 red pepper, julienned
- ½ cup cilantro, rough chopped
- ¼ cup mint leaves, rough chopped
- 2 tablespoons raw cashews, chopped

CASHEW LIME DRESSING

- 1 chiltepe chile (substitute Thai chile)
- 2 garlic cloves
- 2/3 cup fresh lime juice
- 2 tablespoons gluten-free tamari soy sauce
- ¼ cup maple syrup or agave
- 2 tablespoons sesame oil
- ¼ cup olive oil
- ¼ cup water
- 1/3 cup raw cashews

- Prepare all the ingredients for the salad and mix together in a large bowl.
- To make the dressing, blend everything in a high-speed blender until smooth.
- Pour the desired amount of dressing into the salad and toss until well incorporated. Reserve the remaining dressing to use as a dip or dressing for another salad.
- Taste and adjust salt and lime if needed.

Watercress Mandarin Salad
with turmeric vinaigrette
Serves 4

Watercress is literally my favorite green! Not only do I love its light, crisp, peppery flavor, it is also a major superfood - bursting with vitamins and minerals. This aquatic herb, usually found along streams and rivers, is in the Brassica family along with broccoli and cabbage. Once used to prevent scurvy, it has more vitamin C than oranges, more calcium than milk, and more iron than spinach. The perfect detox food, it kickstarts a sluggish metabolism and helps build strength. It's rich in minerals, including significant amounts of iodine, and cleanses the blood. This salad combines zesty citrus, crunchy and aromatic fennel, and a nutritive turmeric dressing that yields a unique umami flavor.

SALAD

- 1 bunch watercress, washed, large stems removed
- 1 mandarin orange or tangerine, segments halved
- 1 medium fennel, thin slices
- 1/8 red onion, thin slices
- 2 tablespoons raw macadamias, rough chopped

VINAIGRETTE

- ½ cup mandarin orange or tangerine juice
- 1-2 inch piece of ginger
- 2 tablespoon apple cider vinegar
- 3 tablespoon avocado oil
- 2 teaspoon turmeric powder
- 1 tablespoon honey
- 1 tablespoon mellow miso
- 2 teaspoon mandarin or tangerine zest
- 1 teaspoon chia seeds
- ¼ teaspoon salt

- In a high-speed blender, blend all ingredients for the vinaigrette until smooth.
- Toss together watercress, orange slices, fennel, and onion.
- Drizzle the vinaigrette over the salad, top with macadamias, and serve.

It is said that Hippocrates, the "Father of Medicine" built his hospitals near rivers so he could easily harvest watercress to nourish his patients.

Central American folklore claims aromatic loroco flowers have aphrodisiac effects. I'll let you be the judge!

Arugula Camote Salad
with Loroco Ranch Dressing
Serves 3-4

You may be familiar with loroco flowers if you've ever eaten Pupusas, the famous El Salvadorian specialty. These small, tightly closed buds appear in the markets in Guatemala around July for just a few months and have a very unique flavor profile. Earthy and herbaceous, loroco also tastes slightly nutty, which inspired me to use it as a base for a vegan ranch dressing – and it's amazing. If you can't find loroco, use pumpkin or sunflower seeds. Sweet camote and spicy arugula complement the intensity of the dressing, while radishes add a nice crunch. Both fresh avocado and it's oil provide healthy fats, creating a well balanced and colorful salad with a fun Guatemalan twist!

SALAD

- 2 medium camote or sweet potato, chopped into ½ inch cubes
- 1 tablespoon coconut oil
- 4 cups baby arugula
- 3 radishes, sliced thinly
- ¼ cup raw walnuts, rough chopped
- ½ avocado, sliced
- handful chopped chives
- amaranth sprouts for garnish
- loroco flowers for garnish

LOROCO RANCH

- 1 ½ cups loroco flowers, rinsed
- 2 tablespoons lemon juice
- 1 ½ tablespoons dried dill
- 1 ½ teaspoons garlic powder
- 1 ½ teaspoons onion powder
- ¼ cup avocado oil
- ½ cup water
- ½ teaspoon mustard (grainy)
- 1 ½ teaspoons sea salt

- In a large skillet heat 1 tablespoon coconut oil on medium heat. Sauté camote plus a few pinches of salt until tender. Set aside.

- Meanwhile, in a high-speed blender, blend all ingredients for the dressing until smooth. Taste and add more salt or lemon if desired. If it's too thick, add a little water.

- In a large serving bowl, combine the arugula, radishes, walnuts, avocado, and camote or sweet potatoes.

- Toss with an adequate amount of dressing. Garnish with amaranth sprouts and more loroco flowers to serve.

4

Mains

Guate Buddha Bowl with Tamarind Peanut Sauce

Basil Macuy Vegan Pesto

Yuca Falafel Fritters

Cozy Butternut Casserole with Nutmeg Cashew Cream

Green Mango Spring Rolls with Cashew Lime Dip

Chillout Chipilín Enchiladas with Avocado Lime Sauce

Guate Buddha Bowl
with Tamarind Peanut Sauce

Makes 2 bowls

A Buddha bowl - while a perfect reminder to cultivate your yogic lifestyle - is just an excuse to drown a salad in peanut sauce! Any combination of veggies works here, and it's always fun to use a variety of colors. Start with a base of gluten-free grains or buckwheat soba noodles. Then add cooked and raw veggies, mushrooms, herbs, sprouts, sesame seeds, and a ferment like sauerkraut for some tangy acidity. A good nut butter sauce takes a Buddha bowl from good to exceptional - this Tamarind Peanut sauce is a winner. Tamarind pulp is used in Guatemala to make a popular refreshing beverage. Considered cooling in Ayurvedic medicine, it's balanced levels of potassium and magnesium make tamarind a great electrolyte drink for fluid loss in hot weather. It has a significant amount of pectin that makes it a great treatment for both diarrhea and constipation. It's easy to start with the pulp, which includes the fibers and seeds, and process it into a thick paste. Find blocks of tamarind pulp in the ethnic section of the grocery store, or any Mexican or Asian market. If you can't find tamarind, the sauce is still delicious without it.

BOWL

- 100g gluten free soba noodles
- 5 shiitake mushrooms, sliced, including stems
- 2 güicoyitos, sliced (or zucchini)
- 2 radishes, sliced handful snap peas
- 2 tablespoons mint leaves, chopped
- ¼ cup kimchi or sauerkraut
- 2 tablespoons sesame seeds
- handful sprouts

TAMARIND SAUCE

- 6 ounces of tamarind seeds/pulp (about 1/3 of the package) or premade paste
- 1 cup hot water
- ½ cup peanut butter
- ½ cup tamari
- ¼ cup lemon juice
- 2 tablespoons sesame oil
- 2 tablespoons rice vinegar
- 2 tablespoons honey
- 2 tablespoons tamarind paste
- 1 inch piece of ginger
- 1 tablespoon water
- 1 teaspoon salt

Buddha Bowl cont....

- Cook the soba noodles according to the directions on the package. Drain with cold water, toss with a dash of sesame oil, and set aside.

- Prepare the tamarind paste - peel tamarind seeds, soak seeds and pulp in boiling water, set aside while you cook, about 15 minutes. If using premade paste, skip this step.

- Heat 1 tablespoon sesame oil in a skillet on medium heat.

- Add sliced shiitakes and sauté a few minutes until moist and softened. Set aside in a small bowl.

- To the same skillet, add sliced güicoyitos and sauté a few minutes until cooked through. Set aside in a small bowl.

- Repeat with the snap peas, sautéing a minute or 2, just until tender. Turn off the heat and set aside.

- To make the tamarind peanut sauce, first strain the tamarind seeds, using your hands to mash it and push it through a fine mesh strainer. (skip if using premade paste)

- Scoop 2 tablespoons of the smooth tamarind paste into a high-speed blender along with the rest of the sauce ingredients, and blend until smooth.

- Assemble the bowls - first place the noodles in a bowl, and arrange each ingredient on top. Drizzle with sauce and serve.

Tamarind pods

Güicoyitos are cute Mayan heirloom squash that look and taste like round zucchini.

Basil Macuy Vegan Pesto

Makes about 1 ½ cups

You won't believe this pesto does not have cheese in it! Everyone who tries it is shocked – it's simple, chock full of healing greens and healthy fats, and it honestly passes for the real thing. Macuy is a native Mayan superfood bursting with nutrition. Sometimes called quilete, a name many Guatemalans use to refer to any weed, it is found in every market and often seen in backyards and country roads. It has a delicate vegetal flavor that compliments the basil well in this pesto. I love using the potent and spicy Guatemalan basil "albahaca morada." I usually choose omega-3 packed walnuts for their soft texture and earthy flavor, but feel free to substitute your favorite nut here. This is the most versatile sauce – serve it with zucchini noodles, roasted veggies, over eggs, on sourdough toast, on pizza or baked potatoes, or as a dip for crudités. The possibilities are endless!

1 ½ cups macuy, packed
1 cup basil, packed
½ cup olive oil
2/3 cup walnuts

3 tablespoons lemon juice
2 garlic cloves
½ tablespoon salt

- In a food processor, combine all the ingredients and process until well combined. I like to keep it a bit chunky.

- Store in an airtight container up to a week.

Substitute any green here for the macuy - spinach, watercress, arugula, kale, pea shoots, amaranth leaves, or chard work well too!

Guatemalan basil

Yuca Falafel Fritters

Makes 12 fritters

I love everything in fritter / muffin form. I also love falafel, but garbanzos have always been difficult for me to digest. Introducing my version of falafel, using yuca root as the base. These versatile gluten and bean free fritters (or "tortitas") are so easy to make, and are a great meal or quick on-the-go snack. Yuca, or cassava root, is an ancestral tuber with fermentable fiber that serves as prebiotic food for our healthy gut bacteria. If you can't find yuca, trying using sweet potato. High-protein almond flour works well here to keep the texture light. Generous amounts of traditional falafel spices make these flavor-packed as well as antioxidant-rich. Enjoy these on their own, or topped with your favorite sauce – mine is this Tahini-Cilantro.

FRITTERS

- 3 cups yuca, peeled and shredded
- 1 cup green onions
- ½ cup almond flour
- ½ cup parsley
- 2 eggs
- 1 tablespoon cumin, ground
- 1 teaspoon coriander, ground
- 1 teaspoon turmeric, ground
- ½ teaspoon paprika, ground
- 1 ½ teaspoon salt

TAHINI CILANTRO DRESSING

- 1/3 cup tahini
- 1/3 cup lemon or lime juice
- 1/3 cup olive oil
- 1/3 cup water
- ¼ cup cilantro, packed
- 1 ¼ teaspoon salt
- 1 garlic clove

- Position a middle rack in the oven and preheat to 375°F.
- With 1 tablespoon olive oil, grease a baking sheet or silicon mat placed on a baking sheet.
- In a mixing bowl, combine all ingredients.
- Using clean hands, mix the contents together well, then scoop heaping tablespoons of packed fritters onto the baking sheet. Sometimes it's easier with wet hands.

Yuca Fritters cont....

- Bake for 30 minutes, then turn over with a spatula. Place back in the oven for an additional five minutes.

- Meanwhile make the dressing. Blend all ingredients in a high-speed blender until very smooth. Add more water to thin if needed.

- When the fritters are done, remove from oven and let cool for five minutes.

- Enjoy the fritters on their own, served as a falafel sandwich, or in a salad, with tahini sauce.

Yuca, an ancestral tuber

Cozy Butternut Casserole
with Nutmeg Cashew Cream
Serves 6

If you're craving cheesy comfort food but prefer to avoid the post-meal carb crash, this is the perfect dish. Layers of earthy butternut squash, sweet caramelized onions, and creamy cashew sauce complement each other perfectly to create magic. I find that adding nutmeg to the sauce harmonizes all the ingredients, bringing exotic complexity to this otherwise simple casserole. Guatemala has a few traditional squashes, but the flavor and texture of butternut are hard to beat, and I'm happy to see it's becoming more available. Butternut squash contains huge amounts of vitamin A and C, both important for a healthy immune system and reducing inflammation. For carnivores, a layer of shredded chicken would work well, but on its own, this casserole is perfectly satisfying as an entrée served with a zesty side salad. This dish is dedicated to my favorite client and now friend Eu who I had the pleasure of cooking for while living in Guatemala. Her loyalty and appreciation for high-vibration food inspired my creativity in the kitchen, and I hope you love this recipe just as much as she does!

CASSEROLE

1 large butternut squash, peeled, and sliced thinly into rounds
3 large yellow onions, medium dice
¼ cup coconut oil

NUTMEG CASHEW CREAM

1 ½ cups raw cashews
1 ¼ cups water
¼ cup coconut oil
¼ cup lemon juice
3 tablespoons nutritional yeast
½ teaspoon nutmeg
1/8 teaspoon pepper
½ tablespoon salt, rounded

- Preheat oven to 400°F.
- Slice onions into a medium dice (about an inch). In a large skillet, heat coconut oil on low-medium heat, and slowly caramelize the onions for 30-45 minutes.

Butternut Casserole cont....

- Blend all ingredients for the cream in a high-speed blender until very smooth. Add more lemon or salt to desired taste.

- Grease a 9x13 casserole pan with coconut oil, and first spread one layer of irregular squash slices onto the bottom (reserve the perfect rounds for the top).

- Spread a thin layer of the cashew cream, followed by another layer of overlapping squash.

- Spread a layer of all the onions.

- Feel free to add a layer of shredded cooked chicken if desired.

- Repeat steps until all the squash is used, then top with a final layer of cream.

- Cover with foil and bake at 400°F 45 minutes.

Green Mango Spring Rolls
with Cashew Lime Dip
Makes 12 rolls

There's something special about these spring rolls. My most requested dish while working as a private chef in Guatemala City, one particular client comes to mind – an adorable 5-year-old girl who gobbled these up to her heart's content. Dozens of orders later, her mom finally decided it was time to learn to make them herself.

The star in this tropical dish is green mango, literally the fruit of the unripe mango. The greener and harder the better, yielding the perfect tartness. Green mango has a higher vitamin C content than ripe mango, and it's sourness increases the secretion of bile, giving your liver a boost and helping with digestion. I love adding chopped raw macadamias to these rolls for an added crunch. Don't skip the red onion – it surprises with a nice sweetness. The Cashew Lime dip is to-die-for! Once you get the hang of working with rice wrappers, these rolls are super easy, and you'll want them as a permanent grab-and-go snack in your fridge.

- 12 large rice spring roll papers
- ¼ cup raw macadamias or cashews, chopped
- 2 bunches of rice noodles (for spring rolls, vermicelli)
- 1 large green mango spiralized or julienned
- 1 red bell pepper, sliced into thin 3 inch strips
- ½ red onion, sliced thin
- 1 cup cilantro leaves, rough chopped
- 1 cup mint leaves, rough chopped

- Prepare the veggies, noodles, and nuts, placing each one in a separate bowl in front of you on the counter.
- In a wide, shallow pan, warm up about 2 inches of water. You want to be able to touch the water without burning your fingers.
- Set aside a large plate or cutting board next to your stove. Wet the surface with a little water.

Green Mango Spring Rolls cont....

- When you are ready to start assembling the rolls, grab 1 rice paper, gripping it with both hands on the top. Submerge it in the water, and rotate it a few times until it is soft. Working quickly, remove the rice paper with both hands and gently place it on the plate or cutting board. Make sure the edges are spread out.
- Toward the bottom of the rice paper in the center, lay out the macadamias, followed by the noodles, mango, red onion, cilantro, and mint.
- Fold the bottom over the veggies, rolling into the center of the rice paper. Fold the sides in then tightly roll all the way. You want the roll as tight as possible.
- Repeat with remaining ingredients.
- Serve with the Cashew Lime Dressing from page 48.

Green mango

Chill Out Chipilín Enchiladas
with Avocado Lime Sauce
Serves 6

When I moved to Guatemala, I was surprised at how different the cuisine was compared to Mexican food. Guatemalan enchiladas are nothing like those of their neighbors! Mine are inspired by both countries, with a healthy plant-based twist. The unique Guatemalan ingredient I use here is the chile cobanero, which lends an intoxicating smokiness to this dish. Hailing from the Alta Verapaz region, this chile is traditionally used to flavor the famous turkey soup called Kaq'ik. I love the famous blue corn tortillas, which are purportedly made out of "criollo" or native corn, rather than GMO corn which accounts for the majority of the corn flour and masa on the market. Chipilín leaf, a wild Mayan superfood, is chock full of nutrients and acts as a gentle sedative. I like to layer everything like a casserole, but the tortillas can be rolled and stuffed if you desire.

RED CHILI SAUCE

- 2 tablespoons olive oil
- 1 yellow onion, chopped
- 6 cloves garlic, chopped
- 2 tablespoons ground cumin
- 2 dried whole pasa chiles (or ancho chiles)
- 1 dried whole guajillo chile
- 4 dried whole cobanero chiles
- 12 roma tomatoes, broiled until blackened (or 28 oz can diced fire-roasted)
- ½ cup water
- 2 teaspoons sea salt

- To make the sauce, heat a 3-quart pot over medium heat. Add the olive oil and onion, gently sauté for 10 minutes.

- Add the garlic and cumin, and sauté a few minutes more.

- Next add the chiles, leaving them whole, plus the tomatoes and their juices, water, and sea salt. Cover and simmer over low heat for about 30 minutes.

- Transfer sauce to a blender and blend until smooth.

Enchiladas cont....

OREGANO CASHEW CREAM	AVOCADO LIME SAUCE
1 cup raw cashews	½ avocado
1 cup water	1 cup cilantro, packed
½ cup olive oil	1/3 cup lime juice
3 sprigs of fresh oregano	1/3 cup olive oil
3 tablespoons lemon juice	1 ½ tablespoons cumin
1 teaspoon salt	1 tablespoon honey
½ teaspoon coriander, ground	¼ cup water
	1 teaspoon salt

- In a high-speed blender, blend all ingredients for the Oregano Cashew Cream until smooth. Taste to make sure the flavors are balanced. It should be well salted, with a hint of oregano.
- In a high-speed blender, blend all ingredients for the Avocado Lime Sauce until silky smooth. Taste to adjust flavors. It should be lime-forward, with a hint of cumin.

Enchiladas cont....

ENCHILADA FILLING

1 tablespoon olive oil	6 cloves garlic, minced
1 medium yellow onion, diced	1 tablespoon cumin
1 teaspoon sea salt	2 tablespoons chili powder
1 red bell pepper, diced	3 cups chipilín leaves, de-stemmed
1 zucchini, in small squares	
1 pound mushrooms, chopped (oysters or shiitakes)	12 blue corn tortillas

- To make the enchilada filling, heat a large skillet over medium heat and add the olive oil. Add the onion and salt, sauté until soft, about 5 minutes.

- Next add the bell pepper, zucchini, and mushrooms, and sauté until veggies are cooked. If a lot of liquid remains, pour it out.

- Next add the garlic, cumin, and chili powder, and sauté a few minutes longer. Add the chipilín leaves and sauté a minute or 2 more. Turn off the heat.

- Preheat oven to 400°F.

- To assemble enchiladas, coat a 9x13 glass casserole dish with olive oil.

- You can choose to assemble these as a casserole in layers (tortillas, veggies, cream, chili sauce, repeat), or the traditional Mexican way by filling each tortilla with the veggie mixture and cream, and topping with more sauce and cream.

- Cover with aluminum foil, bake for 45 minutes. Serve with Avocado Lime sauce.

- Store in an airtight container.

Chipilín leaf is an ancient Mayan wild food with vitamins A & C, calcium, and beta-carotene, as well as a compound that has sedative effects on the nervous system.

Kassia's Guate Chili Powder

Makes about 3/4 cup

Every time I am out to eat with a Guatemalan, after browsing the menu choices they ask the waiter, "pica?" Meaning "is it spicy?" This concern always thoroughly amuses me, seeing that the country is full of a variety of delicious and very spicy chiles! At every market, stalls display barrels of dried pasa, guaque, cobanero, and chiltepe chiles, to name a few. I decided to create my own chili powder with a mix of my three favorite Guatemalan chiles. Chile pasa looks like the more common ancho chile we find in the states, but has notes of cacao and raisin. Chile guaque, or guajillo, is a long smooth red chile with a nice sweet heat. Chile cobanero is tiny yet packs a spicy and smoky punch! I love toasting these chiles, then combining them with onion, garlic, coriander, cumin, and dried orange zest to create a flavorful chili powder that celebrates Guatemala.

5 dried whole pasa chiles
3 dried whole guajillo chiles
6 dried whole cobanero chiles
2 tablespoons onion powder
2 tablespoons garlic powder
2 tablespoons coriander, ground
2 tablespoons cumin, ground
1 tablespoon dried orange zest

- Remove the stems and seeds from the chiles.
- Fill a large skillet with 1 layer of dried chiles. Toast on low heat. When the chiles are starting to smell toasted, and turning dark and crispy, remove from heat.
- Repeat until all chiles are toasted.
- In a food processor or grinder, grind toasted chiles with onion, garlic, coriander, cumin, and dried orange zest.
- Store in an airtight glass jar.

5

Snacks

Amaranth Leaf Dip

Cashew "Queso"

Amaranth Moringa Crackers

Zucchini Ramón Bread

Amaranth Leaf Dip

Makes about 2 cups

If you haven't added amaranth leaves to your diet, now is the time! Deemed the "new kale" by some health experts, this nutritious weed (or superfood – depends on who you ask!) has a bright future. In Guatemala it's called bledo, and can be found at nearly every market. This delicious green is rich in protein, potassium, iron, magnesium, calcium, and folate, as well as vitamins A and C. Enjoying this dip ensures a substantial dose of greens, as well as quality fats from the seeds, coconut, and avocado oil. I love cilantro for it's ability to chelate heavy metals from the body, making this the perfect dip to accompany a cleanse or detox.

1 cup sunflower seeds, soaked in water 6-8 hours, strained

1 cup cilantro

1 cup amaranth leaves, packed (sub any mild leafy green here)

½ cup pumpkin seeds, soaked in water 6-8 hours, strained

¼ cup lemon juice

1/3 cup shredded coconut (or 2/3 fresh coconut meat)

3 celery stalks, chopped

¼ cup avocado oil

1 inch piece of ginger

1 tablespoon sea salt

- In a food processor, combine all the ingredients and pulse until you have a smooth paste.
- If your food processor isn't large enough, do 2 or 3 batches.
- Store in an airtight container 4-5 days.

Roll this dip up in cucumber slices for a cute appetizer!

Amaranth leaf, or bledo, is a mild-flavored wild green that easily replaces spinach or chard in any recipe.

Tecpan, Guatemala

Cashew "Queso"

Makes 1 ½ cups

This dip is hands down my most beloved recipe. I make it for every gathering...and if I don't, you better believe I will hear complaints from my addicted friends. This rich, creamy, cheesy cashew dip will win the heart of even the most hardcore cheese lover. A vegetarian's dietary ally, nutritional yeast provides B vitamins and protein and is also the magic ingredient that gives this dip its cheesy flavor. I like to roast my own red peppers, but you can find them already prepared in any grocery store. Reminiscent of the Southern dish "queso," this cashew dip is awesome served with crudités or a nice loaf of sourdough. Make it for your next party and enjoy the rave reviews!

1 cup raw cashews, soaked at least 1 hour, drained

½ cup nutritional yeast

1 large red bell pepper, roasted, blackened, peeled

3 tablespoons apple cider vinegar

½ cup water

1 garlic clove

1 teaspoon salt

¼ teaspoon chile cobanero or cayenne (depending on your spice tolerance)

- Combine all the ingredients in a blender.
- Blend until a smooth sauce forms, adding a little more water as needed.

Juice from the "cashew apple," the fruit attached to the cashew nut, is antibacterial, a great H. pylori treatment, and an overall digestive tonic for ulcers or gastritis.

Amaranth Moringa Crackers

Makes 48 crackers

These superfood crackers are addicting, and not to mention super easy! Protein-rich amaranth flour, regarded as a sacred nutritious seed in the Mayan ancestral diet, creates a light and crispy texture. Moringa boosts the nutrition to an even higher level, possessing high amounts of vitamin A and C, calcium, potassium, iron, and all essential amino acids. These gluten-free crackers would be a perfect snack for any vegetarian as the synergy of amaranth and moringa provide a well balanced complete protein. I love the flavors of thyme and rosemary, but feel free to experiment with your favorite aromatic herbs!

1 cup amaranth flour
3 tablespoons olive oil
¼ cup water
½ teaspoon baking powder
½ teaspoon garlic powder

1 teaspoon thyme
1 tablespoon fresh rosemary, diced
½ rounded teaspoon salt
1 tablespoon moringa

- Preheat oven to 350°F.
- Place all of the ingredients in a bowl and mix well with your hands. The dough will be pliable and spongy - don't be tempted to add more water.
- Place the ball of dough on top of wax paper and gently knead it a little. If the dough is sticky add a little more flour and knead until smooth.
- Flatten the dough into a rectangle shape and place another piece of wax paper on top.
- Using a rolling pin, roll out the dough to a thickness of 5mm (1/5 of an inch). Remove the top wax paper, and using an oiled sharp knife, score a grid of squares of about 1 ½ inches.
- Place the dough and wax paper on a baking tray. Gently prick each cracker with a fork to prevent them puffing up while baking.
- Bake for 25 minutes, or until golden around the edges. They will crisp up as they cool.

Amaranth fields at IMAP

Moringa trees

Zucchini Ramón Bread

Makes 1 loaf

Who doesn't love a good zucchini bread? Zucchinis grow prolifically in my dad's garden in California, and we're always looking for inventive ways to use it. If you can relate, you'll love this new spin on the classic favorite. I like to use the macadamia-rice flour from a Guatemalan company called Terrae, it lends a nice sweet richness to this bread. You can substitute almond flour if you prefer. I add cacao and ramón nut flour for a boost of antioxidants and nutrients, and a little honey for sweetness. Ramón trees are native to the jungles of Petén in Guatemala and produce nutrient-rich nuts that ancestral Mayan have used as food for thousands of years. This is the perfect way to sneak some veggies into your kid's diets. Serve with butter & a pinch of Himalayan salt!

1 cup macadamia/rice flour from Terrae (or 1 cup almond flour)
¼ cup cacao powder
2 tablespoons ramón flour
½ teaspoon sea salt
½ teaspoon baking soda

2 tablespoons coconut oil, room temp
2 large eggs
¼ cup honey or agave
¼ teaspoon vanilla
½ teaspoon ground cinnamon
¾ cup zucchini, grated

- In a food processor combine macadamia flour, cacao powder, and ramón flour.
- Pulse in salt and baking soda. Add eggs, coconut oil, honey, vanilla, and cinnamon.
- Briefly pulse in zucchini.
- Transfer batter to a greased 6.5 x 4 inch medium loaf pan.
- Bake at 350°F for 35-40 minutes

We need a creature who can love and cry and is made of the stuff of nature. A creature who will cross the breadth of time like a humble walker, like a simple traveler, like a gentle wanderer. A creature capable of thanking us.

— Mayan Creation Myth, Rigoberta Menchú

Lake Petén Itzá, El Remate, Guatemala

6

Ferments

Carrot Turmeric Sauerkraut

Guate Green Kimchi

Lacto-Fermented Radishes

Raw Nut Cheese

Pineapple Ginger Soda

Carrot Turmeric Sauerkraut

Makes about 2 quarts

Sauerkraut has got to be one of the world's most nutritious foods, yet it is incredibly easy to make. I was first introduced to it at Three Stone Hearth, a Community Supported Kitchen in Berkeley where I learned to cook. They have a commitment to nutrient-dense, healing foods, and utilize traditional food preparation, cooking, and preservation techniques to enhance digestibility and nutrient availability of every delicious dish they create. I feel incredibly blessed to have worked at Three Stone, and credit them for my appreciation for the highest quality, truly high-vibration ingredients.

This sauerkraut would be great to eat during cold and flu season, featuring immune boosting garlic, ginger, and turmeric and spicy mustard to help expel mucus. I like to let my kraut ferment at least 4 weeks to allow the healing probiotic bacteria to multiply. As with all fermented foods, a little with every meal boosts digestion, feeds your healthy gut bacteria, and helps maintain a balanced gut flora - therefore promoting healthy immunity, combating allergies, energizing cells, and cultivating overall wellness (to name just a few benefits!).

- 2 white cabbages, sliced thin
- 1 large carrot, shredded
- 4 cloves garlic, diced
- 2 tablespoons shredded ginger
- 2 tablespoons grainy mustard (or 3 tablespoons whole mustard seeds)
- 2 tablespoons turmeric powder (or 3 tablespoons fresh, shredded)
- 1 teaspoon black pepper, ground
- 3-5 tablespoons sea salt (depending on size of cabbages)

- Slice cabbage into quarters. Remove the core from each segment, and slice thinly. Add to a large bowl. Add salt, starting with 3 tablespoons.

- Massage the salt into the cabbage a few minutes with your hands, taste and adjust as needed. It should taste just salty enough for you to feel it's "too salty." Continue massaging until the cabbage becomes soft and breaks down enough to release it's juices (also called brine).

Carrot Turmeric Sauerkraut cont....

- Add carrot, garlic, ginger, mustard, and turmeric, and incorporate.

- Stuff the veggies into a clean glass jar, pounding them with your hand or a wooden kraut pounder.

- Cover with as much brine to completely cover the veggies, and add water if needed. You want the veggies under the brine to prevent mold from forming. Leave at least 1 inch of space below the top in case it expands.

- Cover the jar with a ferment airlock lid or towel, securing with a rubber band.

- Let sit out at room temperature to ferment 2-4 weeks, depending on your preference. The longer it ferments, it gets less salty, more sour, & more medicinal!

- Once the kraut is finished, put a tight lid on the jar and move to the fridge.

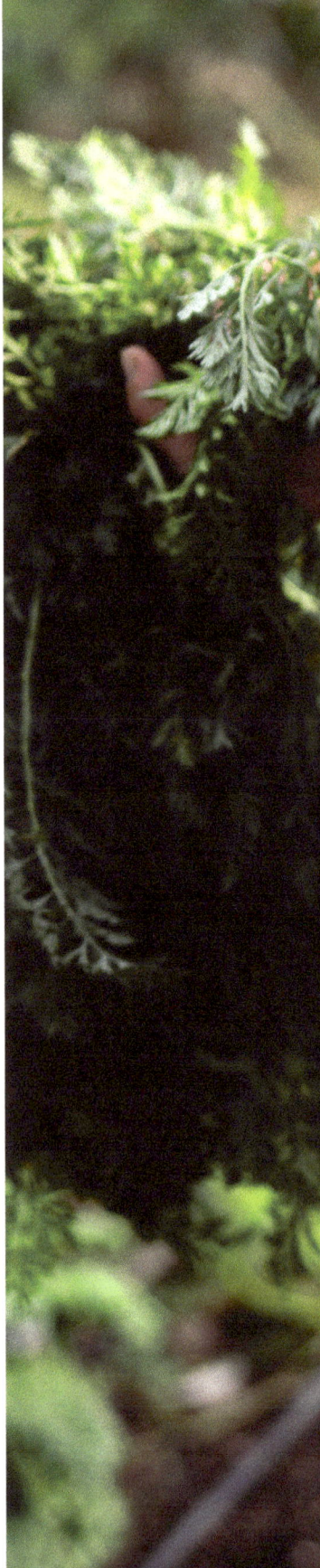

Guatemalans love their spicy little chiltepe chiles!

Guate Green Kimchi

Makes about 2 quarts

Kimchi is a traditional spicy Korean ferment using chiles, garlic, ginger, onion, radish, and cabbage. There's an interesting paradox I found in Guatemala - most Guatemalans can't handle spicy food, yet they adore their local chiltepe chiles and typically will eat them prepared in a hot sauce. I wanted to create a chiltepe based Kimchi, featuring the highly nutritious Mayan superfood chaya. Known as "Mayan spinach," this wild green used to be a staple food of Pre-Colonial peoples, but as with many ancient medicinal foods, knowledge is being lost. Guatemala is one of the most malnourished of all countries - yet one of the most abundant and fertile lands in the world. Some indigenous are losing the connection to the knowledge of their ancestors, and being tempted by the ease, low-cost, & flashy marketing of fast food and packaged snacks lacking in nutrients. Chaya is considered "nature's solution to malnutrition" - it is super high in protein, has 2x the iron as spinach, more calcium than any other veggie, and vitamins A, C, and folic acid - all essential for health. Thankfully, there are organizations dedicated to re-introducing this incredible food to the people of Guatemala. I found that using local chiliecobanero instead of the traditional gochugaru in this Kimchi lends incredible depth and a little smokiness.

- 2 pounds bok choy, chopped into large 2 inch pieces (white and green parts)
- 3 daikon or 30 radishes, sliced very thin or shredded
- 6 tablespoons salt
- 3 oz ginger, rough chopped (¾ cup)
- 1 red onion, quartered
- 8 cloves garlic
- 10 chiltepe chiles
- 12 green onions, (white and green parts) chopped
- 1 cup chaya leaves
- 1 teaspoon fish sauce (vegetarians use 1 sheet of nori)
- 1 teaspoon chile cobanero paste

Serve a few tablespoons of Kimchi as a condiment alongside each meal daily and support your digestion, immunity, and overall wellness.

It's important to cook chaya for at least 10 minutes in a non-aluminum pot to break down the toxic cyanogenic glycosides.

Guate Green Kimchi cont....

- Place the bok choy, radish, and salt in a large bowl or tub. Using your hands, massage the salt into the veggies until they starts to soften a bit.
- Add water to cover the bok choy and radish. Put a plate on top and weigh them down with something heavy, like a large jar. Let stand for 1 to 2 hours.
- Meanwhile, simmer the chaya leaves in a non-reactive pot for about 10 minutes until wilted. Drain.
- In a food processor, combine the ginger, red onion, garlic, chiltepes, green onion, chaya leaves, fish sauce, and chili coban. Process until a smooth paste forms.
- Drain the bok choy and radish over a colander.
- Gently squeeze any remaining water from the bok choy and radish and return them to the large bowl along with the spicy paste.
- Using your hands, gently work the paste into the vegetables. Gloves are useful (but not necessary) to protect your hands from stings, stains, and smells!
- Pack the kimchi into a 2-quart mason jar (or 2 quart jars), pressing down until the brine covers the vegetables. Leave at least 1 inch of space below the top in case it expands. If you have a ferment weight, use it to keep the kimchi below the brine.
- Cover with a towel & secure with a rubber band. Alternately, use ferment lids with airlocks.
- Let the jar stand at room temperature for 2-4 weeks.
- Check the kimchi daily to make sure the veggies stay under the brine. You can use a wooden spoon or clean fingers to press them down again. Sometimes it's a good idea to keep a plate under the jar in case the kimchi expands and liquid leaks out.
- Taste the kimchi after a week or 2 to see how it's coming along. When it tastes sour enough to your liking, you can transfer to the refrigerator.

Lacto-fermented Radishes

Makes 1 quart

If you're a farmer, you know the struggle – you are blessed with a huge harvest and can't keep up with all the veggies! Fermentation is the perfect solution for preserving your bounty and enjoying these veggies all year around. Lacto-fermentation is the oldest form of food preservation used in most ancient cultures across the globe. Lacto refers to the lactobacillus bacteria that thrive when we create an environment free from oxygen. Any veggie can be fermented, and only requires a simple brine of salt and water to create this anaerobic environment for friendly bacteria to multiply. With time, the lactobacillus converts sugars in the veggies to lactic acid, which preserves the food and creates that signature sour flavor! Since lactobacillus is one of the most abundant bacterias found in our guts, it's clear that fermented veggies should be a daily part of our diets to support gut health.

Here is a simple recipe for fermented radish that can be used for any veggie you like. I prefer a pure brine, but feel free to get creative with spices and flavors you enjoy. I use the resulting fermented brine to culture my nut cheeses.

BASIC BRINE
3 tablespoons SALT : 1 quart WATER

½ quart (2 cups) warm purified water

1 ½ tablespoons sea salt (free of anti-caking agents & iodine)

1-2 pounds radishes, quartered

1 quart jar

OPTIONAL SPICES:

1-2 garlic cloves

½ teaspoon coriander seeds whole

½ teaspoon caraway seeds

½-1 teaspoon turmeric powder

¼ teaspoon peppercorns whole

½ teaspoon dill

1 tablespoon grated ginger

Be creative – experiment with spice combinations!

Any veggie works with this recipe - cauliflower, carrots, beets, green beans, zucchini, cucumbers - the possibilities are endless!

Lacto-fermented Radishes cont....

- Cut radishes into fourths, or if making pickles, leave whole or quartered.
- Make brine - combine salt and water, and make sure it dissolves.
- First add your spices and garlic to the jar, then the veggies - pack them tightly.
- Pour the brine over the veggies, leaving 1-2 inches from the top of the jar.
- Make sure the brine is covering your veggies completely.
- Cover the jar with a ferment airlock lid or towel, securing with a rubber band.
- Let sit out at room temperature to ferment 2-4 weeks, depending on your preference!
- The longer it ferments, the less salty and more medicinal it gets!

Raw Fermented Nut Cheese

Makes 1 round

I'll never forget the first time I tried nut cheese at one of the original raw food restaurants, Roxanne's in Marin County, California. It was 2004, I had stumbled upon Roxanne's gorgeous cookbook, RAW, and immediately became mesmerized by the living foods lifestyle. Roxanne's raw creations were true culinary art, and her restaurant was a gourmet experience for any foodie who appreciated high vibrational food. Dinner was a splurge for me back then, but worth every penny – I still can taste her incredibly smooth herbed cashew cheese, which was a revelation at that time. Roxanne used rejuvelac from fermented wheat berries to cure her cheeses. I've seen a trend of using probiotic capsules, which gets the job done quickly, but I prefer the slow process of naturally curing my cheeses with lacto-fermented brine from fermented veggies. This process allows you to appreciate how precious this cheese is with each bite. Experiment with adding herbs, miso, nutritional yeast, or spices to create your own piece of culinary art!

1 cup raw cashews or macadamias, soaked overnight or 8 hours

¼ - ½ cup fermented liquid (brine from any fermented veggies)

½ teaspoon Himalayan salt

about 3 tablespoons powdered moringa and oregano, combined, as a rind

OPTIONAL SEASONINGS:

¼ cup fresh diced herbs – basil, thyme, oregano, parsley

2-3 tablespoons nutritional yeast

1-2 tablespoons miso paste

1-2 teaspoons garlic powder

2-3 tablespoons diced shallot or red onion

1-2 tablespoons lemon juice

more salt as needed

- Drain the nuts.
- In a Vitamix or high-speed blender, blend the nuts, brine, and salt. Keep adding brine until a very smooth paste forms, almost the consistency of a thick cream.

Cashews make the smoothest raw cheese, but macadamias are amazing as well!

Raw Fermented Nut Cheese cont....

- Place the mixture in the center of a large piece of cheesecloth or thin towel. Gather it tightly, and tie it with a string.

- Place a sieve or strainer over a bowl and transfer the cheese bundle into the sieve.

- Top with a heavy stone or jar, pressing down the mixture, allowing the liquid to extract. Leave in a warm place to ripen for 24-48 hours (depending upon your taste for sourness).

- Remove the cheese from the cloth. Mix in optional savory ingredients if you desire.

- Shape the paste into a round cheese shape. If you desire, roll the cheese in the powdered herbs, creating a rind.

- The cheese can be eaten from this point, but if you prefer a more firm texture, follow these instructions:

- Drape a new piece of cheesecloth or a towel over a small plate. Place the cheese round on top of the plate, draping the cloth delicately over the cheese.

- Place in the refrigerator to dry out for a few days. The texture will be more of a spreadable cheese, rather than a true hard cheese.

- Cheese is best eaten within 10 days.

Fermented Pineapple Ginger Soda
(Fresco de Súchiles)

Makes 4 cups

Nearly every traditional culture in the world has at least one way of preserving a food through fermentation. Guatemala has just a few, and the first that was introduced to me was Fresco de Súchiles. One day while teaching a cooking class to a client's cocinera (or house cook), I noticed she was reserving all our leftover pineapple skins. She explained she was going to use them to make a beverage with sugar and spices. I later learned that this was actually a fermented drink, which piqued my curiosity! Similar to the Mexican Tepache, which is typically made with cinnamon, the Guatemalan version is a mishmash of many spices and other seasonal fruits and is usually made during Semana Santa, or Holy Week (Easter).

The friendly bacteria in soda fermentation typically need sugar to reproduce – the soda becomes tart as the sugars are digested. I use panela, which is raw, unrefined sugar cane and still contains nutrients, unlike white sugar. Cardamom, allspice, and ginger prevent bloating, while the enzyme bromelain in pineapple aids digestion, making this your go-to drink for gut health!

½ pineapple, cut into chunks (leave skin on)

90 g ginger (about 1 cup), chopped into large slices

¼ c panela (substitute Rapadura or brown sugar)

20 allspice seeds, whole

1 teaspoon cardamom, whole

4 cups purified water

½ gallon jar

- Wash the pineapple and then cut it into chunks.
- Mix the sugar and water until the sugar dissolves.
- Gently break up allspice and cardamom in a mortar and pestle (do not powder).
- Add the pineapple chunks, ginger, allspice, cardamom, and sugar water to a large glass jar or pitcher.

- Cover with a cotton cloth or towel and secure with a rubber band (or use ferment airlock lid), & store on the counter in a cool, dry place for 4-6 days, until it starts to bubble.
- If a layer of foam forms, scoop it out. When sufficiently fermented to your level of sourness, strain, & store covered in the refrigerator. If you prefer more bubbles, strain into an airtight bottle, such as a plastic water bottle, and let sit out another day or 2 until the carbonation builds up.
- Serve chilled.

Baby pineapple

When given the chance to thrive, a plant will emerge into its own perfect version of itself. We are just like plants – we are each born with our own seed of innate wisdom to activate our higher purpose.

– Kassia Fiedor

7

Desserts

Hibiscus Lime Tarts

Almond Ramón Cookies

Peanut Amaranth Alegría

Coco Camote Cupcakes

Cardamom Orange Truffles

Hibiscus Lime Tarts

Makes 10 8-cm tarts

"Rosa de Jamaica" is a popular refreshing drink in every Guatemalan kitchen made from Hibiscus sabdariffa, also known as Roselle or Jamaican sorrel. This particular hibiscus is high in antioxidants and as a diuretic, it has shown very promising results to naturally lower blood pressure. Its tart flavor is evidence of a high vitamin C content and works very well in these pretty treats. Macadamia nuts, boasting heart-healthy fats, are abundant in Guatemala and work perfectly here as a base, but feel free to substitute any other nut.

BASE

- 1 cup macadamia nuts
- 1 ¼ cup dates
- ½ cup shredded coconut
- 2 tablespoons puffed amaranth
- ¼ teaspoon vanilla

FILLING

- 1 ½ cups full fat coconut milk
- ½ cup lime juice
- ½ cup honey or agave
- 8 dried hibiscus flowers (or powdered)
- 1 tablespoon zest of lime
- 2 teaspoons gelatin

- Sprinkle a little shredded coconut onto the bottom of each tart pan.

- In a food processor, grind macadamia nuts until almost powdered. Add dates, coconut, amaranth, and vanilla and process until a thick paste forms.

- Press the paste into the tart pans to form a crust for each tart.

- Pour all ingredients for the filling into a small pot and stir well. Let it sit for 3-5 minutes so the gelatin can "bloom."

- On medium heat, warm the bloomed filling mixture, stirring vigorously until it comes to a boil.

- Remove from heat and strain the liquid into a glass jar that pours easily.

- Fill the prepared tarts, and put in the refrigerator for a few hours or overnight to firm up.

Don't let the fancy presentation fool you – these tarts are super easy to make!

Wild hibiscus in El Paredón, Guatemala

Macadamia nuts

Almond Ramón Cookies

Makes 10 cookies

These cookies will be your new favorite! Free from gluten, dairy, and refined sugar, they're a healthy treat for you or your kiddo. High-protein, low-carb almond flour is my go-to baking flour, and ramón nut flour lends a hearty dose of nutrients. I like to use cacao powder and dark chocolate chips for a double dose of antioxidants and minerals, as well as the carminative spices cardamom and cinnamon to support digestion (and for incredible flavor). Kid tested, mother approved!

¾ cup almond flour
2 tablespoons ramón flour
2 tablespoons cacao powder
¼ teaspoon salt
¼ teaspoon baking soda
¼ teaspoon cardamom

¼ teaspoon cinnamon
1/8 teaspoon vanilla powder (or ¼ teaspoon vanilla extract)
¼ cup coconut oil, melted
¼ cup maple syrup
¼ cup chocolate chips

- Preheat oven to 350°F.
- Combine dry ingredients in a medium size bowl. Stir to mix well.
- In a small bowl or Pyrex measuring cup, combine melted coconut oil and maple syrup. Stir to combine, and then pour into the bowl with the dry ingredients. Mix to incorporate, making sure to break up the balls of almond flour.
- Spoon out 1 heaping tablespoon per cookie, and form into balls with your hands.
- Place them on a baking sheet lined with a silicon mat, or greased with butter, then gently press down to about 2 inch diameter. Leave at least an inch between each cookie as they will spread out during cooking.
- Press a few chocolate chips into the top of each cookie.
- Bake for 20 minutes. They will get crisp up as they cool to room temperature.

Ramón flour is an incredibly nutritious ancestral superfood - ramón trees are native to Central and South America, and the nut was once a staple in the ancient Mayan diet.

Ramón nuts drying

Majestic Ramón trees

Peanut Amaranth Alegría

Makes about 10 small bars

The most beautiful lake in the world, Lago Atitlán in Guatemala, is home to a Taoist monastery that produces the best peanut butter I've tasted in my life. Tucked up on a steep hillside in the village of San Marcos lies a simple yet elegant temple overlooking the stunning volcano-lined lake. The gentle monks spend their days meditating, practicing Tai Chi, and farming coffee, peanuts, and other fruits on their lush property. They infuse their training with precision, care, and contemplation into each step of the production of their products, creating an incredibly high-vibration peanut butter so divinely creamy I eat it by the spoonful. These nutrient-dense sweet treats are inspired by alegría, the traditional Mexican amaranth candy. Cinnamon, cardamom, and orange zest lend their digestive supporting carminative powers, while maca supports energy and hormonal balance. Enjoy these joyful treats when you need a nutritious energizing pick-me-up.

½ cup natural peanut butter
1/3 cup honey
1 tablespoon coconut oil
1 teaspoon cinnamon
¼ teaspoon cardamom
½ tablespoon maca
1 teaspoon orange zest
1/8 teaspoon Himalayan salt
1 ¼ cup puffed amaranth

- Spread plastic wrap or parchment paper into an 8" x 8" brownie pan.
- In a small pot on low heat, warm the peanut butter, honey, coconut oil, cinnamon, cardamom, maca, zest, and salt. Stir constantly until everything is incorporated.
- Add the amaranth, quickly mixing it with the peanut butter paste.
- Immediately pour it into the prepared pan, spreading out a smooth layer.
- Chill in the refrigerator, then cut into squares.
- Store in the refrigerator until ready to eat.

Fresh honeycomb at
La Colmena de Don Antonio

PRECAUCIÓN
APIARIO A 100 M.

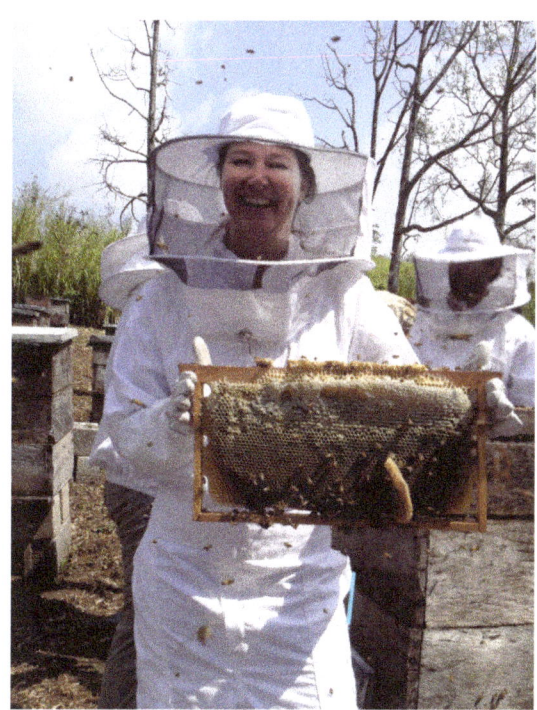

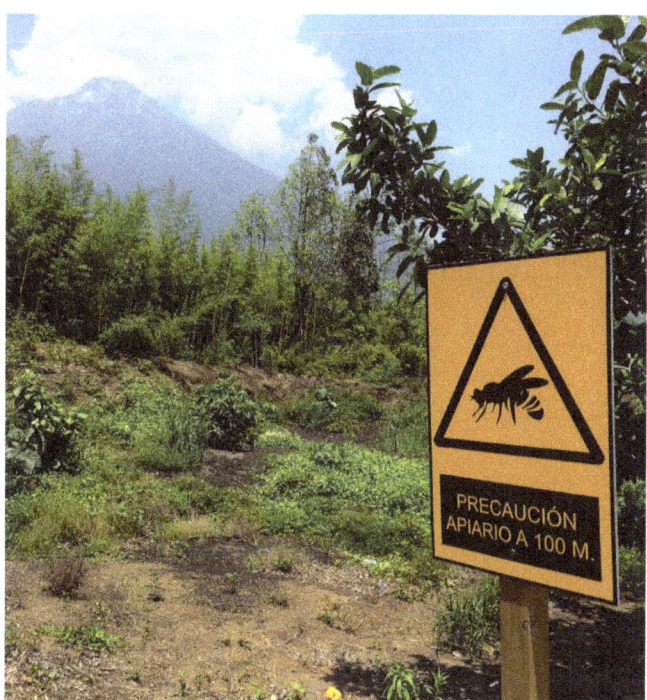

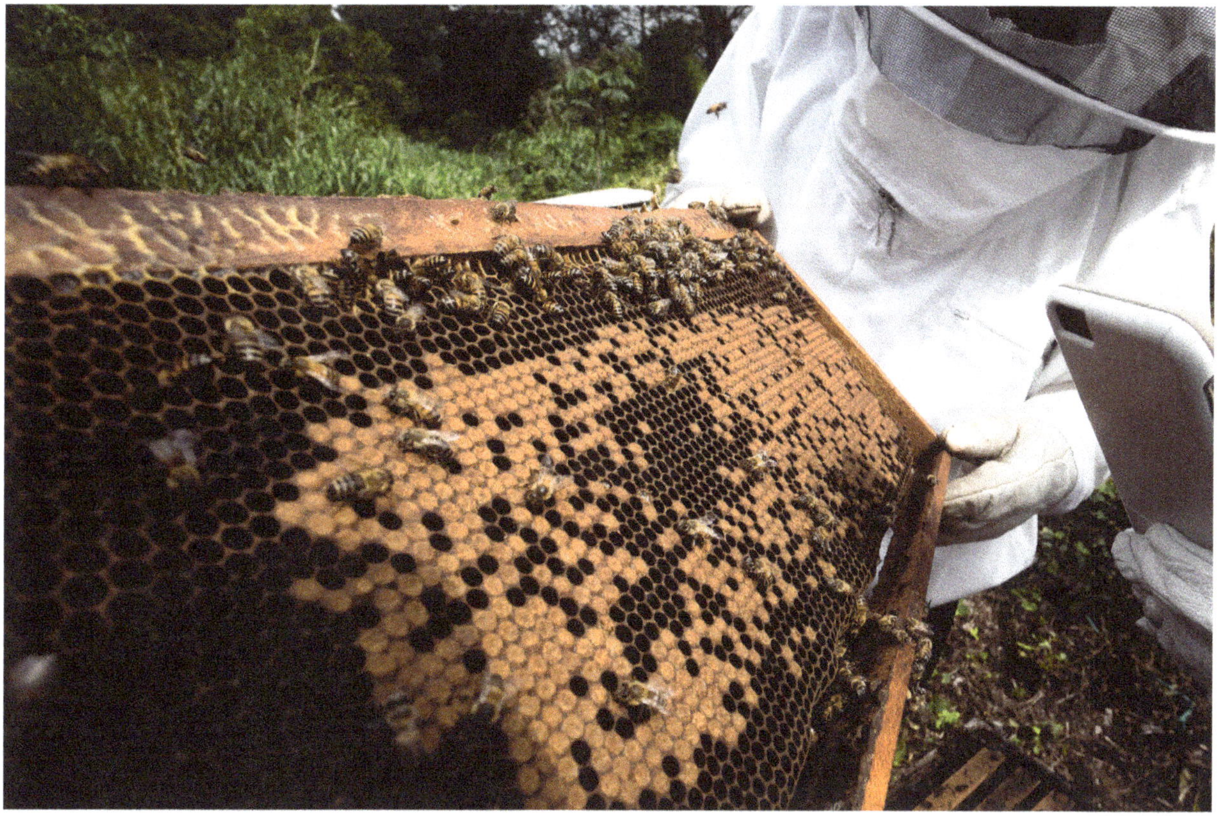

Coco Camote Cupcakes

Makes 14 small cupcakes

Sometimes we need easy, tasty ways of sneaking veggies into our diet. These cupcakes are a great way to do that! Guatemala's signature sweet potato, the camote, provides fiber, antioxidants, vitamins, and minerals. It's also a great source of resistant starch, which feeds the good bacteria in our gut and has been shown to help regulate blood glucose levels, improving insulin sensitivity. Coconut flour is one of the healthiest gluten-free flours out there - low in carbs, non-inflammatory, low glycemic, and full of healthy fats. Carrot or any winter squash will work perfectly if you don't have sweet potato. I make these often to serve as breakfast muffins, but topping them with the Cashew Orange Frosting makes them an extra special gluten-free dessert!

CUPCAKES

- 1 cup coconut flour
- 1 cup shredded camote
- 2 teaspoons cinnamon or pumpkin pie spice
- ½ teaspoon ground cardamom
- ¼ teaspoon salt
- ½ teaspoon baking soda
- 8 eggs, at room temperature
- ½ cup softened butter or coconut oil
- ¼ cup + 2 tablespoons raw honey or pure maple syrup
- 1 teaspoon vanilla extract
- 2 teaspoons apple cider vinegar

CASHEW ORANGE FROSTING

- 1 cup cashews, soaked at least 1 hour
- 2 tablespoons coconut milk
- 3 tablespoons honey
- ¼ cup coconut oil
- 2 tablespoons orange juice
- zest of ½ orange (or 1 drop orange essential oil)
- 2 pinches Himalayan salt

- Preheat oven to 350°F and line 14 small muffin cups with liners. The non-stick silicone muffin molds work well here.

- In a large bowl, combine coconut flour, camote, spices, salt, and baking soda. Mix well.

- In a medium size bowl, beat eggs, then add oil, honey, vanilla, and vinegar. Pour wet ingredients into the dry ingredients, stir to incorporate.
- Pour the mixture into prepared muffin molds.
- Bake for about 25-30 minutes, until golden and the top springs back when lightly pressed.
- Meanwhile, make the frosting. In a high-speed blender, blend frosting ingredients using a plunger to push everything down until cashews are smooth. The frosting will be thick!
- Cool the cupcakes a few minutes, then top with frosting. Store in the fridge.

Cardamom Orange Truffles

Makes about 16 truffles

If you're looking for something that tastes decadent and elevates your soul, then these high-vibe chocolate treats are perfect. Macadamias are high in fiber, manganese, and B1, and of course heart-healthy fats! They're also naturally low in phytates, so they don't require soaking or sprouting to make them more digestible. And even if grown conventionally, they don't need a lot of pesticides, so don't stress if you can't find organic. Dates provide a ton of fiber, allowing the sugars to slowly absorb, preventing a dreaded sugar spike. These truffles contain a nice therapeutic dose of cacao, which is a powerhouse of antioxidants that improve mood, boost libido, and increase mental clarity. Cardamom, cinnamon, vanilla, and orange zest aid in digestion and impart an alluring, sensual aroma. Maca adds even more sexiness by strengthening your vital force while balancing hormones. Feed your erotic spirit with these heart-opening truffles, or make some for your sweetie as a token of your love!

- 1 cup macadamias
- 60 g hard chocolate (1/4 c), melted
- 1 tablespoon coconut oil, melted
- 1 ½ cups dates
- ¼ cup cacao, ground
- ½ teaspoon cardamom, ground
- ½ teaspoon cinnamon, ground
- ¼ teaspoon vanilla powder
- ½ tablespoon maca
- 1 teaspoon orange zest or 2 drops essential oil
- 1/3 teaspoon salt

- In a food processor, process macadamia nuts until finely ground.
- Melt the hard chocolate and coconut oil together in a glass jar in the microwave or stove.
- Add all the ingredients to the ground macadamias, process until well combined. The mixture will start to form a ball.
- Using about 1 tablespoon mixture for each truffle, form into balls using your hands.
- If rolling in toppings, drop the balls into a shallow bowl or Tupperware covered with shredded coconut, orange zest, or cacao powder, and roll them around to coat.
- Store in the refrigerator.

Cacao freshly harvested at Hacienda Rio Dulce

Cacao pod exposing fresh beans

8

Drinks

Amaranth Mint Green Smoothie

Tropical Turmeric Smoothie

Choco-Zapote Smoothie

Ramón Nut Latte

Petén Chai

Third Eye Moringa Latte

Turmeric Orange Macadamia Milk

Mayan Hot Chocolate

Amaranth Mint Green Smoothie

Serves 2-3

This smoothie evokes a tropical fantasy of relaxing on a white-sand beach, sipping a Pina-Colada. You won't get buzzed, but you'll get a little kick from nutrient-dense superfoods like amaranth leaves, moringa, and chia. Amaranth leaves, or bledo in Spanish, are a rich source of iron, magnesium, calcium, and folate. Moringa packs a nutrient punch with significant amounts of protein, calcium, and iron to name a few. Chia adds more plant-based protein and omega-3's while emulsifying the mixture, allowing you to make this smoothie the night before and grab-and-go the next morning.

1 cup coconut milk
1 cup water
½ cup amaranth leaves (bledo)
1 cup pineapple
2 teaspoons moringa

3 teaspoons lemon
16 leaves of fresh mint
2 teaspoons chia
2 tablespoons protein powder, stevia, or honey to sweeten

- Add all ingredients to a high-speed blender, and blend until smooth and creamy.

Native Guatemalan bananas

Tropical Turmeric Smoothie

Serves 2

Here in Guatemala, mango trees grow prolifically across the country. When it's mango season, roadside stands and vendors pop up everywhere, selling bushels of all varieties! This time of year you can feel more joy in everyone's spirits, because who doesn't love these perfect delectable fruits? In this smoothie, the flavors of rich creamy coconut combined with the sweet tang of mango are a match made in heaven, while the hint of cardamom makes this smoothie exotic and sexy. Anti-inflammatory turmeric increases the medicinal value, making this your go-to smoothie when you're lucky enough to have mangos in your life! Tip – chop and freeze your mangos so you can enjoy them all year long!

1 cup coconut milk (or any non-dairy milk)

½ cup frozen mango

1 tablespoon chia seeds

juice of ½ a lemon

¼ teaspoon ground cardamom

½ teaspoon ground turmeric (or 1 inch fresh root)

honey or agave to taste (between 1-3 tablespoons)

optional: scoop of your favorite plain protein powder

- Add all ingredients to a high-speed blender, and blend until smooth and creamy.

Choco-Zapote Smoothie

Serves 2

Mamey sapote, or zapote fruit is the star in this nutrient-rich smoothie. An ancient Mayan delicacy, this pink-orange salmon colored fruit is high in vitamin A, potassium, and fiber, and the taste is reminiscent of sweet potato pie! Combining it with banana, cacao, maca, and macadamias creates a milkshake-like texture, and leaves you feeling full and energized for hours. A few dates lend sweetness to this smoothie while boosting fiber and won't cause a sugar spike. Add a little smokey chile cobanero or cayenne pepper to create some Mayan vibes!

1 ½ cups water
1 frozen banana
3-4 dates
1 tablespoon macadamias
½ mamey sapote

2 tablespoons cacao powder
2 teaspoons maca
1 tablespoon chia seed
pinch of chile cobanero

- **Add all ingredients to a high-speed blender, and blend until smooth and creamy.**

Ramón Nut Latte

Serves 1

Infuse your morning with the spirit of the Mayan jungle! The ramón tree is indigenous to Central and South America and the Caribbean, and the nut was once a staple in the ancient Mayan diet. In Guatemala, it's ground up and made into a porridge-like drink called "atol" or added to tortilla flour. Ramón is highly nutritious – rich in fiber and calcium, as well as a great source of protein, potassium, and iron! Roasted, it really does have a rich coffee-like feel and taste. As a galactogogue that increases milk production, it's a perfect caffeine-free drink for pregnant and breast-feeding women.

In Petén, near the famous pyramids of Tikal, I visited a ramón processing facility run by a collective of 50 women. Also part of the collective are 200 nut collectors who live in the Maya Biosphere Reserve where these 120-foot trees grow. The ripe nut falls to the ground, and collectors are instructed to leave about 20% of the nuts for animals and new seedlings. In such a rural area, this collective provides a great opportunity for jobs in the community, making ramón an incredibly sustainable and ethical plant to support! You can buy ramón, or Maya nut in the states from a fabulous company called Jnantik.

- 2 teaspoons ramón coffee alternative (roasted ramón flour)
- ½ cup hot water
- ¾ cup hot coconut milk
- ½ teaspoon cinnamon
- pinch cardamom
- 1 tablespoon maple syrup or honey
- 1 teaspoon maca

- Heat the water and coconut milk in a small pot.
- Add everything to a blender and blend on high until smooth.
- Strain if desired.
- Alternatively, you can premake your ramón coffee in a French press or drip, and then blend it with all the other ingredients.

Tikal Mayan temples in Petén

Petén Chai

Makes about 10 servings

During cooler weather, this warming tea will keep you feeling cozy and also gently stoke your digestive fire. These aromatic, carminative spices are packed with antioxidants and antimicrobial compounds that boost immunity and protect us from pathogens, while also preventing gas and bloating. Allspice trees grow wild in the jungles of Guatemala, and are said to produce some of the finest allspice berries in the world. You've probably smelled the exotic and stimulating scent of the berries, but the fresh leaves are just as lovely! When visiting Petén, I picked the leaves off the tree and infused them in hot water to make a simple digestive tea. If you are lucky enough to come across fresh allspice trees, use the leaves for this recipe, otherwise, you probably have allspice berries in your kitchen already! Make a big batch of this concentrate and enjoy it with your whole family.

6 cups water
3 cinnamon sticks
3 inches ginger, cut in large slices
12 allspice berries or 2 allspice leaves
2 teaspoons cardamom seeds
5 peppercorns
1 tablespoon orange peel
nut milk
honey or sweetener of choice

- Simmer the water, cinnamon, ginger, allspice, cardamom, peppercorns, & orange peel in a large pot for an hour, covered.

- Strain the tea – this is your concentrate.

- To prepare a cup, mix 1 part concentrate with 1 part nut milk and add honey to your liking.

- Alternatively, you can premix an entire batch & store in your fridge. Heat when ready to enjoy, then add sweetener of choice.

Third Eye Moringa Latte

Serves 1

Craving a nourishing warm drink, but not the caffeine? This latte will lift your spirits and get you through the afternoon slump. Moringa, originally from India but perfectly adapted to the tropical climate of Guatemala, is a major superfood gaining esteem in the wellness world. It contains tyrosine, an amino acid that increases mental alertness and focus. According to VieMoringa, an artisan producer in Guatemala, moringa contains 10 times more vitamin A than carrots, 15 times more potassium than bananas, 25 times more iron than spinach, 9 times more protein than yogurt, and 17 times more calcium than milk. The healthy fats in the macadamia milk allow better absorption of the fat-soluble vitamins in the moringa, while uplifting mint aids digestion. Add a touch of honey for sweetness, and enjoy.

1 teaspoon moringa powder
1 cup macadamia milk
3 mint leaves
honey to taste

- Heat macadamia milk in a pot, then add to a high-speed blender with moringa, mint, and honey.
- Blend until smooth and creamy, strain if desired.

Moringa has been touted as an effective herb for "decalcifying" the pineal gland because of it's use in purifying flouridated and toxic water.

Turmeric Orange Macadamia Milk

Serves 4

The Golden Milk craze was fun, but how about we switch it up a bit? We're all looking for easy ways to add more healing turmeric into our daily routine, and this recipe does the trick. I start by soaking raw macadamias, which are abundant in Guatemala, overnight. I then blend the nuts with the turmeric, spices, orange juice, and honey and strain to create a large batch of medicinal macadamia milk. I prefer to use fresh turmeric root, which is bursting with nutritive compounds to fight inflammation, boost immunity, ease digestion, heal wounds, and sooth joint pain. Adding black pepper increases its bioavailability. Turmeric can taste very earthy, so adding in aromatic spices like ginger, cardamom, and vanilla not only make this tasty but also supports a healthy digestion. Enjoy this chilled or at room temperature.

1 cup macadamias, soaked overnight, strained

3 cups purified water

2 tablespoons fresh turmeric root, or 1 tablespoon powdered

1 inch piece of ginger

½ teaspoon cardamom

½ teaspoon vanilla powder

3 tablespoons orange juice

2-3 black peppercorns (or ¼ teaspoon ground)

2 tablespoons honey (or to taste)

- **Blend all together in a high-speed blender, and strain. Store in your fridge and serve cold.**

Mayan Hot Chocolate

Serves 1

Some people will tell you that Guatemala is the birthplace of chocolate. For over 4,000 years, people in Central and South America have harvested this mystical bean, using it ceremonially as food and medicine, and even as currency. The ancient Mayans had a deep daily connection with cacao, understanding it as a part of their creation myth, and considered it the "food of the Gods." Today across the globe, we are still honoring this divine superfood for its numerous healing gifts. The flavonoids in cacao are mood-elevating, gently stimulating, and yet calming to anxiety. This sense of euphoria may explain why many consider cacao to be an aphrodisiac. It's very common to see cacao sold in blocks or discs in Guatemala – these are used to make a hot chocolate drink. Most contain high amounts of sugar, but if you're lucky you will find pure cacao, or at least 85%. Allspice, indigenous to the Guatemalan jungles of Petén, was a popular spice used by the ancestors to flavor hot chocolate and creates a cozy warm feeling. It's intoxicating fragrance is reminiscent of cinnamon, nutmeg, and clove. Sip a steaming cup of this decadent elixir, and offer up a prayer of gratitude to the cacao god Ek Chuah, who will ensure abundant cacao harvests for years to come.

- 1 cup boiling water
- 20 g 100% cacao bar or dics (or about 3 tablespoons chopped)
- 1 tablespoon macadamia nuts
- ¼ teaspoon allspice
- pinch of chile cobanero or cayenne
- ½ teaspoon maca powder
- 1-2 tablespoons maple syrup

- Blend everything in a high-speed blender until frothy and smooth. Strain first if you desire.

Heirloom cacao

Raw cacao beans & bars

Featured Farms

Michelle B. Sultán founded La Botica Verde as Guatemala's premier online ecological supermarket. The company delivers fresh, local, organic foods, ecological cleaning supplies, natural cosmetics, and zero-waste products. All vegetables are grown locally by small and medium size farmers and hand-picked the day before delivery. La Botica cultivates relationships with each farmer they work with, and visits the farms directly to ensure organic practices. They have a zero-waste policy & use reusable or biodegradable packaging, showing their commitment to the planet.

La Colmena de Don Antonio (Mr. Antonio's Hive) was founded in 2014 by Luis Eduardo Girón. Being the third generation of beekeepers, he has honored his grandfather's passion for beekeeping naming the brand with his name and producing honey in three different regions of Guatemala. Luis has also diversified the business by opening an apitourism and native-bees conservation project showing and teaching visitors biodynamic beekeeping techniques. Colmena's ethical and compassionate treatment of their bees, agro-forestry projects, raw extraction, & care for the environment all come together to create an incredibly high quality honey.

Juan Bronson's farm, Hacienda Rio Dulce is a part of one of the oldest fincas in Guatemala. The original "Finca Fronteras" was largely deforested of hardwoods during WWII and when Juan's grandmother acquired the land in 1973 it was being used as a cattle ranch. His family started collaborating with the environmental authorities to protect the existing stands of natural forest, and over the last 3 decades has regenerated all of the pastureland with endangered, tropical hardwoods while maintaining habitat. As of 2010, Juan has established cacao and other shade crops on the forest floor to create cash-flow and add biodiversity to their systems. Hacienda Rio Dulce features native species and heirloom varietals of cacao.

Juan Orellana is a self taught investigator-developer-farmer, from Guatemala. He synergistically combines the world of mechanics, agriculture, and health. 20 years experimenting with veganism, raw-food, fruitarianism & coaching others on their health journeys inspired Juan & his wife Ligia to develop AgroFenomenal, an Organic Agro-Practice. He culminates nature observation and learning from progressive scientists teaching alternative perspectives to create a system that goes beyond biodynamic. The AgroFenomenal system is based on getting closer to the natural laws of plants and soil, with the intervention of a key re-mineralization of the soil with direct marine sources. He also incorporates energy that draws upon the magic of the universe, like fields, light & sound, while infusing love into everything he does. His incredibly high vibration vegetables are a true reflection of this beautiful system - as seen in the spiral farm on the opposite page. He is currently consulting farmers to cultivate their farms with the AgroFenomenal system.

Featured Farms

In a world of immense beauty & abundance, Giuliana Gobbato's life purpose is finding ways for humanity to be of service to our global ecosystem - living in ways that create more life, habitat, and joy. Her company Garden Greens exists soul-ly for this purpose, changing the food system through sustainable land management. They teach talented farmers ways to produce more bounty in respectful & intelligent ways. PILAS agriculture means smart agriculture, the acronym in Spanish stands for: Polyculture, Integrated, Local, Food Sovereignty, and Health; this is the backbone of their beyond-organic approach. Giuliana has created a new model for selling produce that benefits farmers instead of middle-men. By going straight to conscious restaurants, they can plan production based on needs, which maximizes profit & minimizes food waste. Restaurants get produce that is organic, Earth gets more trees and clean rivers, & the farmers get a higher income, beautiful food for their families, and the joy of knowing they are making a new future possible.

Qachuu Aloom, which means "Mother Earth," is an association formed by indigenous Mayan in Rabinal to promote community development and strengthen individual and collective capacities through traditional & organic agriculture. Magdalena Alvarado leads the group of women who have united to grow organic amaranth. After they lost their husbands and their villages in the war in Guatemala, Magdalena was determined to create opportunity for herself & other widows. Through their seed bank, they are able to rescue a variety of native seeds, including sacred amaranth. By incorporating traditional Mayan ceremonies, educating on nutrition, & selling their products, these women are now rebuilding, empowering, & nourishing their communities. Currently Qachuu Aloom has 500 members, 80% of which are women.

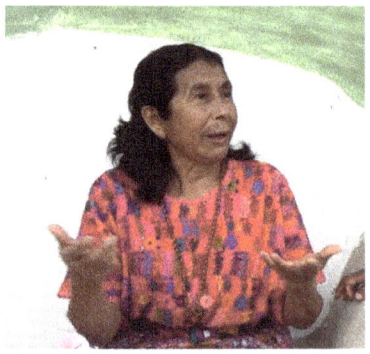

The Mesoamerican Permaculture Institute (Instituto Mesoamericano de Permacultura - IMAP) is a non-profit organization based in Lake Atitlán, Guatemala. It was founded in 2000 as an ecological education center to promote permaculture techniques, local biodiversity conservation, production of organic food, and has a seed bank that strives to preserve the Mayan seed heritage. IMAP's vision is to create food sovereignty & self-sustaining communities by providing permaculture education and ancestral Mayan knowledge, through the safeguarding of their native seeds and their local ecosystems. They offer community service, workshops, certified permaculture courses, tours, group trips, school trips and consultations.

Shan Ren Farms is an intentional community of monastics and practitioners of the Way, living together on the hillside of Lake Atitlán. These monks are passionate about their gardens of coffee, jocote, and peanuts, and use organic farming techniques that follow nature's ways and rhythms. They train rigorously in precision, care, patience and contemplation, and carry this meditative practice into the growing and making of their artisan products. Their peanut butter is heavenly!

Somewhere within our bloodline, our ancestry, within our DNA itself, there was someone who lived in accordance with the vital intelligence of Nature and the spirit of the Earth. And as we heal ourselves down to the roots of who we are, that healing spreads outwards to the branches, leaves and flowers of our family tree, touching upon our lineage. Through our own healing work, we can come into contact with the true nature inside of us that is connected to the true nature outside of us, reclaiming our connection to the vital intelligence of the Earth.

— Sajah Popham

Acknowledgments

Thank you to everyone who contributed to this project!

TABLEWARE & HOME GOODS

Corinne
www.corinneregalos.com

Meso Goods
hwww.mesogoods.com

Itza Wood
www.itzawood.com

Maya Loom
www.mayaloom.com

The Conscious Home / MEEMA
www.meema.co

Ines Farias

EMOTIONAL SUPPORT

Kevin OnenO Hastings

Lisa Fox

Alyssa Hyndman

Lily Acevedo

Kathy & Richard Fiedor

Hilary Golbin

Melissa Alonzo

Paola Rojas

Masumi Patzel

Jarmilka Hanek

ORIGINAL CONCEPT

Lucia Barrios

PRINCIPLE PHOTOGRAPHY

Mono del Espacio
www.monodelespacio.com

ADDITIONAL PHOTOGRAPHY

Mandala Photo
www.mandalaphotoguate.com

Hacienda Rio Dulce / Izabal Agro-Forest
www.izabalagroforest.com

Garden Greens
www.instagram.com/enverdece

Jnantik Ancient Mayan Superfood
www.jnantik.com

Etnica Fair Trade
www.etnicasc.com

La Colmena de Don Antonio
www.instagram.com/colmenadonantonio

ORGANIC PRODUCE

La Botica Verde
www.botica-verde.com

Finca Moran
www.instagram.com/fincamoran

Caoba Farms
www.caobafarms.com

Index

A
Allspice, 20, 128, 168, 176
Almond flour, 68, 104, 133, 138
Amaranth, 13, 16, 18, 19, 20, 24, 27, 54, 65, 91, 92, 94, 100, 102, 133, 134, 142, 155, 156, 182, 188
Amaranth leaf, 91, 92, 94, 156
Arugula, 54, 65
Avocado, 50, 54, 59, 80, 83, 84, 92

B
Banana, 158, 162, 170
Berro, (see watercress)
Bledo, (see amaranth leaf)
Bok Choy, 116, 119
Butternut squash, 59, 72, 75

C
Cacao, 86, 104, 138, 150, 152, 153, 162, 176, 178, 179, 180
Camote, 13, 20, 29, 30, 31, 32, 45, 54, 133, 148
Cardamom, 13, 16, 19, 24, 128, 133, 138, 142, 148, 150, 160, 164, 168, 174
Cashew, 16, 19, 34, 48, 59, 72, 75, 76, 78, 83, 91, 96, 98, 124, 125, 148, 149
Chaya, 116, 118, 119, 188
Chia, 13, 22, 24, 27, 50, 156, 160, 162
Chili cobanero, 14, 80, 86, 96, 116, 162, 176
Chili pimiento, 14
Chiltepe, 48, 86, 114, 116, 119
Chipilin, 13, 14, 59, 80, 84, 85
Coconut, 16, 20, 22, 27, 42, 45, 48, 92, 134, 148, 156, 160, 164

E
Eggs (cage-free, huevos de patio), 14, 16, 19, 64, 68, 104, 148, 149

G
Guajillo chili, 80, 86
Guicoyito, 29, 36, 60, 62, 63

H
Hibiscus, 13, 16, 19, 133, 134, 136
Honey, 16, 22, 24, 30, 31, 50, 60, 83, 104, 134, 142, 146, 148, 149, 156, 160, 164, 168, 170, 174, 181, 188

I
Ichintal, 29, 36

K
Kimchi, 60, 109, 116, 117, 119

L
Loroco, 45, 52, 54

M
Maca, 20, 22, 34, 50, 76, 78, 104, 124, 125, 134, 137, 142, 150, 155, 162, 164, 170, 174, 176
Macadamia, 22, 34, 50, 76, 78, 104, 124, 125, 134, 137, 150, 155, 162, 170, 174, 176
Macuy, 36, 38, 59, 64, 65
Mamey sapote, 155, 162
Mango, 45, 48, 59, 76, 78, 79, 160
Maple syrup, 16, 19, 20, 24, 48, 138, 148, 164, 176
Moringa, 91, 100, 103, 124, 155, 156, 170, 173

N
Nutritional yeast, 72, 96, 124

P
Panela, 128
Pasa chili, 80, 86
Peanut butter, 59, 60, 62, 133, 142, 182
Pineapple, 109, 128, 130, 156

R
Ramon, 91, 104, 133, 138, 139, 140, 141, 155, 164, 188

S
Sauerkraut, 60, 109, 110, 112
Shiitake, 40, 84
Soba noodles, 60, 62

T
Tahini, 68, 70
Tamarillo, (see tomate de arbol)
Tamarind, 13, 24, 26, 27, 48, 59, 60, 62
Tomate de arbol, 24, 27
Turmeric, 40, 42, 45, 50, 68, 109, 110, 112, 120, 155, 160, 174

W
Watercress, 40, 45, 50, 51, 65

Y
Yuca, 59, 68, 70

Z
Zapote, (see mamey sapote)

Bibliography

Ayales, Adriana. "Decalcify your pineal gland with these herbs." Animamundi Herbals. 5 Dec, 2018. https://animamundiherbals.com/blogs/news/decalcify-your-pineal-gland-with-these-herbs

Badore, Margaret. "Reviving the ramón nut: An ancient food offers new hope for fighting malnutrition." Tree Hugger. 2 October, 2018. https://www.treehugger.com/green-food/reviving-ramon-nut-ancient-food-staple-offers-new-hope-fighting-malnutrition.html

Brody, Jane. "Ancient, Forgotten Plant Now 'Grain of the Future.'" NY Times. 2 November, 2018. https://www.nytimes.com/1984/10/16/science/ancient-forgotten-plant-now-grain-of-the-future.html

Cáceres, Armando. Plantas de Uso Medicinal en Guatemala. Guatemala City: Editorial Universitaria, Universidad de San Carlos de Guatemala. 1999.

Gaitán, María Elena. "Foods From The Americas: Amaranth, The Outlaw Grain." East of the LA River. 15 Nov 2018 http://eastoflariver.blogspot.com/2008/05/amaranth.html

Hellmuth, Nicholas M. Maya Ethnobotany Complete Inventory. Guatemala: FLAAR Reports, 2014.

Jung, CG. **C.G. Jung Letters, Vol. 1: 1906-1950.** Princeton: Princeton University Press, 1992.

Kimmerer, Robin Wall. **Braiding Sweetgrass: Indigenous Wisdom, Scientific Knowledge and the Teachings of Plants.** Minneapolis: Milkweed Editions, 2013. Copyright ©2013 by Robin Wall Kimmerer. Quote reprinted with permission from Milkweed Editions.

Matsumoto, Nancy. "Why Mexican Chefs, Farmers And Activists Are Reviving The Ancient Grain Amaranth." National Public Radio. 5 Sept, 2018 https://www.npr.org/sections/thesalt/2017/05/01/526033083/why-mexican-chefs-farmers-and-activists-are-reviving-the-ancient-grain-amaranth

Menchu, Rigoberta. **The Honey Jar.** Toronto: Groundwood Books, 2006.

O'Connor, Amber M. **3,000 Years of the Mayan Hearth.** Maryland: Rowman and Littlefield, 2017.

Rainforest Alliance. "Flour Power: The Mighty Ramón Nut." 10 Sept, 2018. https://www.rainforest-alliance.org/pictures/flour-power

Rose, Victoria. "Chaya Factsheet." Guatemala, Universidad del Valle de Guatemala. Biodiversity International. 2017 http://www.nuscommunity.org/fileadmin/templates/nuscommunity.org/upload/documents/Publications/2017_Chaya_fact_sheet_May15__2__compressed.pdf

Schlesinger, Victoria. **Animals and Plants of the Ancient Maya: A Guide.** University of Texas Press; 1st Edition, 2002.

Vélez-Jiménez E, Tenbergen K, Santiago PD, Cardador-Martínez MA. Functional Attributes of Amaranth. Austin J Nutri Food Sci. 2014;2(1): 1010.

Zavala, Katherine. "Guatemalan Amaranth and Vegetable Soup." Thousand Currents. 14 Nov, 2018 https://thousandcurrents.org/guatemalan-amaranth-and-vegetable-soup/

About the Author

Kassia Emily Fiedor is a Holistic Nutritionist, Herbalist, and Private Chef from Southern California. Passionate about using plants, herbs, & vegetables as medicine, she encourages her clients to eat in harmony with their bodies and nature. Kassia lived in Guatemala for 5 years where she taught healthy cooking classes and made nutrient-dense meals for people with an appreciation for nourishing high-vibration food. Amazed by the abundance of native superfoods, she fostered intimate connections with small organic farmers and artisans producing high-quality products.

Kassia infuses ancestral ingredients into healing plant-based dishes in her debut cookbook, **Cocina Holistica**. Drawing upon the magnificent beauty of Guatemala, she hopes to inspire renewed respect for indigenous foods in creative, modern recipes.

Kassia honors her teachers - David Crow, Cheryl Fromholzer, William Siff, Catherine Abby Rich, Rosemary Gladstar, Jane Bothwell, 7song, Paul Bergner, Tami Grooney, & Gail Julian.

Connect with Kassia on Instagram @infusedholistickitchen

Love my book? As an independent author, your Amazon review helps me so much!

Hold your phone's camera over this code
to leave a review on Amazon

Tag your posts!
#COCINAHOLISTICAGT

Hold your phone's camera over this code
to visit @infusedholistickitchen

www.ingramcontent.com/pod-product-compliance
Lightning Source LLC
Chambersburg PA
CBHW040356010526
44108CB00049B/2921